Secrets

By:
Jonathan

Secrets
Book Eight of the Series *The Nine*
May 22, 2018, *First Edition*

Copyright © 2018

Cover Photo Credit: Nate Hobi

All rights reserved. This book or any portion thereof may not be reproduced or used in any manner whatsoever without the express written permission of the publisher except for the use of brief quotations in a book review or scholarly journal.

ISBN-13: 978-1-942967-36-1

KreativeMinds Publishing
www.kreativeminds.net

Ordering Information:

Special discounts are available on quantity purchases by corporations, associations, educators, and others. For details, contact the publisher at the above listed address or the email address below.

U.S. trade bookstores and wholesalers: Please use the email address below. email: publishing@kreativeminds.net

Unto His Grand Glory, through whom all things are possible.

Always,
Jonathan

Introduction

...

This book is divided into 3 parts – each part yielding an ocean of truth to be explored. While each section may seem uncomplicated on the surface level, the wealth of information contained can be studied for a lifetime. The first section entitled "Pillars" explains how the mind, body, and spirit work together in harmony. This section is fundamental to every aspect of life and must be understood in the soul and applied through the action of the body rather than understood in the brain and applied through action. The second section entitled "Foundation Stones" disambiguates how language was formed and how thought manifests. This is the age-old scientific question about thought answered in the motion of the pillars. Finally, the section entitled "Song of the Spheres" explains the most sacred and holy of principles: it is the explanation of All That Is and how the human experience came to be. It is the fabric of life, the fabric of the aether. It is the architecture of All That Is. It is Glory. It is Love.

Always,
Jonathan

...

Invocation

This will be the last thing written in closure of this book, for it is the first thing that will be read in opening of the words about to forth come. For in closure of writing these words is the opening of these words to another. These words are offered unto all in The Truth, but also as a metaphorical offering of the Octaval Sphere in knowledge to all that has been imparted through His infinite Wisdom. For in the end is the beginning for another; an opportunity to transcend octaves of understanding, consciousness and spirituality. An opportunity to find a closer bond with the Great Almighty.

Lord, our Father – the observance of the simple gifts You have bestowed unto mankind in the great expanse of All That Is is merely a penitence in our earthly recognition to the abundance of divinity's calling – an expanse of offering far greater than the human mind can rationally comprehend. In the observance of simplicity, a greater understanding to the complexity in simplicity's divine creation becomes apparent. The hardest thought to fathom is often the simplest to understand. And herein, the human mind has the great challenge to discern the elegance and grace within the simple to better understand the majestic divinity from which all that Your hand has allowed to be.

Secrets

The world is observed through the senses, captured with the eyes, communicated through the mouth, and experienced through the emotions the mind calls upon the body. Rarely does man stop to rationalize the irrationality of the experience as observed through the ego. And therein lies the greatest challenge to the observer: the ability to remove the veil to existence and understand how Your Spirit moves through all living things – as all living things are only a portion of the Great Spirit. Perhaps the ego is a necessary victim created by the senses – for if the senses did not exist with the extensive clarity as understood through the eyes of mankind, the mind would have less information to discern its individuality from the whole. Or perhaps if the ego was only privy to a portion of the senses, the same trials and tribulations would exist because the rationalization of the experience would only be in the earliest stages of learning and development. But, perhaps an even greater amount of information exposed through the senses would create more confusion through obfuscation of Your Great Truth.

So perhaps, the clarity found in the simplicity of creation should be seen unto mankind as Your greatest gift of all. For in the simple truths observed, an elegance unstated speaks to the soul. And within that elegance, a simple truth expounded unfolds as a miracle of understanding in All That Is, All That Was, and All That Will Be. Unquestionably, thought will be disrupted from the truths spoken herein. But as these words have been impressed upon my soul and have been called into action by Your Grace through Thy own hand, may The Spirit

Invocation

of All That Is fill the hearts and minds of those who read these words and seek Thee in humility. As it was and as we are asked to do, for in it is as my spirit is called to do, I humbly offer these words unto You.

...

Your Grace expounded.
Gravity calling.
All my Love unfolded unto You.
Amen.

...

PART 1

Pillars

Introduction to Pillars

Within these pages are words to meditate by – to focus and find clarity within. Each word is rooted in an essence that permeates the being. Unto its own, each word is more than meaning – each word is motion. Within that motion, a certain resonance, phrasing, rise & fall of thoughts enraptures the spirit so the meaning becomes more than the literal. Take pause to contemplate the richness of the words and allow the mind to travel across the cosmos in exploring their essence. In time, these words will give rise to the archetypal concepts of being, awaken the contemplator and remove the great veil to those seeking reason but who yield in reverence to Divine answer. Life is predicated on these archetypal concepts. In the origin of man and the birth of communication, these twenty-two words formed the pillars to All – All That Was, All That Is, and All That Will Be. Let this forever henceforth be known as the Grand Design of the Twenty-Two.

Each of the twenty-two pillars can be explored alone, or with the accompaniment of the linguistic history that these pillars are found embedded within. It is His will that these pillars be demonstrated through ancient Hebrew, though they can be applied to nearly every ancient language throughout history.

Secrets

For if ancient Hebrew is studied first, the application of the pillars to other languages can be understood. If other forms of language are studied first, the meanings are skewed and distorted before being applied back to Hebrew.

As each pillar is discussed, the left hand page will show the evolution of the pillar in glyph form. Think of each glyph as a way to notate the twenty-two archetypal concepts of thought. Above the glyphs, the name of the letter is given. This is similar to how, in English, children learn the alphabet by saying "a is for apple, b is for banana, etc." However, each letter in Hebrew only has a name for the letter, and is not referred to as the letter itself. The letter holds meaning in the name of the letter, thus how each letter represents a pillar – an archetype of divine thought.

The top-most glyph represents the earliest form of Hebrew known to mankind today. This form of Hebrew is referred to as Early Semitic and was used from the origin of language until approximately 1200 BCE. The second glyph represents another form of Early Semitic used around the same time, but differs slightly in visual representation due to the linguistic evolution that occurred. The third glyph is referred to as Paleo-Hebrew and originated around 1200 BCE. It was used through the first century CE. The fourth glyph is the Moabite script found on the Moabite Stone. It is virtually identical to Paleo-Hebrew and was the written form of the Moabites in 840 BCE. The fifth glyph is the Hebrew script used on the Great Isaiah Scroll, discovered in the find of the Dead Sea Scrolls. It is one of the oldest Dead Sea Scrolls and

Part 1 | Pillars

dates back to approximately 125 BCE. The sixth and final glyph is the modern Hebrew-Aramaic version of the pillar. This glyph is how modern Hebrew is currently written and represents a merging of Aramaic and ancient Hebrew.

In understanding these pillars at an archetypal level, the brain is able to begin to assimilate the Divine language of God. The reason that the oldest religious texts disclose that nothing should be added or taken away from their original writings is because the most divine, archetypal interpretation of thought is conveyed through the architecture of the words themselves. Every word and every letter contains multiple levels of meaning. Nothing should ever be taken literally or accepted as truth at the surface level alone. This very concept breaks the thought of how most of humanity has been taught to learn. Mankind, today, communicates linearly and therefore accepts words by definition. This is the greatest flaw in the interpretation of every religion. For, every religion houses the same truths. The lens of the scribe may have colored or distorted the truths slightly, but the overarching message is the same. The greatest education for mankind should not be in accepting religious truths, but rather *how* to accept religious truths. These same pillars even transcend science from binary thought to archetypal thought, when applied through Part 3 of this book.

It should come as no surprise that the most ancient religious texts state that mankind will one day return to the most ancient of languages in the End of Days. This is because the most ancient languages hold within them divine truths – and the true intention bound within the words of God. It does not

Secrets

mean that each person must be fluent in the original languages of mankind, but rather that the archetypal pillars must be understood in order to hear God's voice. As one begins to progress through understanding the pillars, notice should be taken that the pillars only hold seven fundamental constructs/motions. The seven constructs/motions are applied to the mind, the body, and the spirit uniquely. The application of the seven constructs/motions to the three building blocks of existence form the first twenty-one pillars. They can be studied in grid-form if needed to help visualize the multi-dimensionality in the meanings. The final pillar is to be studied alone, for it is most representative of freewill and how one applies the first twenty-one pillars to his walk.

Observe the truths in the pillars. It is imperative that Part 2 of this book be read after reading Part 1, in order to find understanding in how the pillars find motion and express truth. For just as a circle has no beginning and no end, humans find themselves attempting to understand a circle of truth linearly. But when there is no beginning and no end to the truths held within this book, one must hold the truths of "Pillars" and the truths of "Foundation Stones" together before one can truly understand each of the pillars alone. Together these concepts form a circle of understanding. Part 3 further extrapolates the ideas of the pillars and foundation stones in motion, but one is not required to understand the principles of Parts 1 & 2 in order to understand Part 3. However, no section in this book can be wholly understood on its own. Seek to apply all of the principles of the pillars to the other sections of the book, and the

Part 1 | Pillars

other sections of the book to Pillars. It is only within the study of this book in its entirety that the divine message housed within these pages can truly be understood.

Of The Mind

The words of the Mind should not be thought of as a relationship to the physical brain – or even the thoughts that occur within the brain. The Mind should be conceived as the construct of All That Is and All That Was. The brain should be recognized as the interpreter of the Mind realized through the body and the invocation of the spirit; the words of the mind should be recognized as the foundational archetypal constructs used in understanding the human experience. The mind is a melding of yin and yang, but through which yang is the measured dominant leaving the construct of the mind to gravitate toward the masculine – though it is the embodiment of both the masculine and the feminine definitions. Masculine and feminine could better be defined as dominance and subservience (rather than gender), though both dominance and subservience must co-dependently exist for the archetype to be manifest.

...

Secrets

Of The Mind
Ancient Hebrew – "Aleph"
...

1. Strength

Part 1 | Pillars

1. Strength

Strength is the first, the beginning, the primordial descriptor of that which has no description. Before anything can happen, strength must first be present. Whether it is words, action, rest – strength is the construct of everything that could be manifested, enclosed in a silent & infinite veneer – the heavenly foundation. This word knows no boundaries as strength can be realized through anything that is. But before anything can be, strength must have first been present – the omniscient almighty, the foundation upon creation. It is the first concept; the first number; an odd number; masculine to the concept of yang; a concept humans can understand to exist, but not fully understand its existence.

...

Secrets

Of The Mind
Ancient Hebrew – "Beyt"
...

2. House

Part 1 | Pillars

2. *House*

House is the second concept, the illustration of structure. The house is the encompassing archetype that can hold within it strength. It is the yin to strength's yang. The house is the embodiment through which strength can be demonstrated to exist in the human experience. If this archetype did not exist, strength would cease to be recognized because it would return us to the archetypal concept of everything – equidistant in being – knowing no beginning and no end. House represents the second number; an even number; feminine in polarity because it could not exist without strength, but strength could not be understood without the concept of the embodiment of a house.

...

Secrets

Of The Mind
Ancient Hebrew – "Gimel"
...

3. Abundance

Part 1 | Pillars

3. Abundance

The concept of abundance could also be understood as wealth, but the latter contains connotations of physical wealth. Abundance is best seen as a measurement, but more importantly a ratio to that which is not lacking abundance. In the progression of the archetypal mind, it is the means by which strength can be measured – where strength represents any construct of foundational content. Strength is the core – the beginning – and is representative of anything, so abundance is representative of the measurement of anything that is; the cup that floweth over. Abundance is the third concept; it is the third number; an odd number; masculine; a measurement of something that already is, so it represents the dominant concept to the measurement of what is not .

...

Secrets

Of The Mind
Ancient Hebrew – "Dalet"

...

4. Potential

Part 1 | Pillars

4. Potential

The yin to abundance's yang, potential, is the fourth archetypal concept. Once abundance has been understood to be a construct defined by something which can be measured, the recognition of the lack of that particular something has been defined. Potential is always smaller in measurement to abundance but does not represent an absolute ratio to abundance. Potential represents an absolute ratio to the concept of strength. Abundance is only proportional to potential by definition of that which can be given unto the other. Potential is the fourth concept; the fourth number; an even number; feminine due to it being initially defined by the existence of the construct of abundance, but is thereby the concept that defines how much abundance exists in proportion to all that could be.

...

Secrets

Of The Mind
Ancient Hebrew – "Hey"
...

5. Revelation

Part 1 | Pillars

5. Revelation

Revelation is the outward expression of movement. From rest, an archetypal concept must be moved in one direction or another. The human experience dictates that direction is defined by cardinality (North, South, East, West) or by geometric axis (X, Y, Z). But to understand the archetypal construct of revelation, one must understand that through the first four archetypes, space has not yet been defined. The only archetypal concepts that have been defined are to be understood through the lens of equidistance (which is the single most complicated concept to understand, but the most simple to know once it has been defined). For now, just think of equidistance as an infinitely sized sphere, no corners, no definition of shape. So with that visualization, the archetypes discussed so far have only defined that which is. So now for motion to take place, a concept must only grow or shrink equidistantly. Since infinite strength is the great foundation to All That Is, the only direction that could ever be conceived is equidistant expansion – otherwise infinity would be finite. Through equidistant expansion, the archetype of revelation has been manifested. Revelation is not limited to the action of revealing, but rather the action of expression; growth; to burst forth. Revelation is the fifth concept; the fifth number; an odd number; masculine; a descriptor of the action of outward movement of expression.

...

Secrets

Of The Mind
Ancient Hebrew – "Vav"

...

Y

Y

⪍

Y

ו

ו

6. Nail

Part 1 | Pillars

6. Nail

Since within the progression of the archetypal concepts the outward movement of expression has been contemplated, the inward movement of expression has now become manifest. The nail is a representation of this archetypal concept – to drive in; to hold together; to bind; to sink into. A nail is the inward expression of motion – the inverse of revelation. A nail is the yin to revelation's yang. If something can be put forth, it can now be placed within. A nail is the sixth concept; the sixth number; an even number; feminine in nature because it cannot be observed in construct without the understanding of revelation, but now is the concept in which revelation must hold a relative proportion.

...

Secrets

Of The Mind
Ancient Hebrew – "Zayin"
...

7. Plow

7. *Plow*

When plow is meditated upon, it can be understood that a plow is a tool, an action, or a method through which to do work. The seventh and final archetypal concept of the mind should be viewed as just that – an actionable method of intent through movement. A plow is a way to bring action unto a medium. If a form was never plowed, it would be smooth and without form. The Earth would not even exist without the ability to be opened up for receipt from the mind. In the same way a plow is used to prepare the Earth to receive seeds, everything that is manifested in the human experience must have once been open to receipt of the mind's intention. A plow is the most primal archetype of intention in movement. To plow is to meld all of the first six archetypal concepts into existence and motion, and deliver the concept of actionable intent through which the as-of-yet unexplored archetypal concepts can take root and grow. Plow is the seventh concept; the seventh number; an odd number, masculine in existence; the action of the mind; it is dependent on the first six concepts which are counter dependent on it to apply forth the motion and intent thereof.

...

Of The Body

The words of the Body should be thought of as a relationship to the physical embodiment of the Mind. If the Mind is conceived as the construct of All That Is and All That Was, the Body should be recognized as the physical embodiment and vessel for the Mind. Like the Mind, the Body is a melding of yin and yang, but through which yin is the measured dominant leaving the construct of the Body to gravitate toward the Feminine – though it does embody both the masculine and the feminine definitions. As gender is equated to dominance and subservience, the Body is subservient to the Mind.

...

Secrets

Of The Body
Ancient Hebrew – "Chet"
...

8. Yoke

Part 1 | Pillars

1. *Yoke*

The yoke is a concept through which different meanings are to be meditated upon and a common bond is to be learned. A yoke can be seen as a divider – a fence-like structure. But a yoke could also be seen as an item that joins through division. This is demonstrated through the concept of a yoke holding two oxen. The yoke keeps the oxen separated by a defined distance, but holds them together so they work in harmony. A yoke is not just a divider, and it is not just an object that joins. A yoke is a bond that joins, but maintains separation. The yoke is the eighth archetypal concept, the first archetype of the body. It is the physical manifestation of the first archetype of the mind. Yoke is the bond that must be understood first before it can be embodied in the physical plane. Yoke is analogous to the first archetype of the mind. It is to the body in the way strength is to the mind. Yoke has no form. Yoke is the eighth archetype; the eighth number; an even number; the first archetype of the body; feminine by number, but yang to the division of the Body; a concept that is the very definition through which the body can exist.

...

Secrets

Of The Body
Ancient Hebrew – "Tet"
...

9. Embodiment

Part 1 | Pillars

2. Embodiment

Embodiment is the archetypal concept of the container by which a yoke can be defined. Embodiment can be interpreted to be the human body, but should more specifically be understood as the physical manifestation of form. For form to exist, there must first be a concept for it to contain. The concept contained within the body is the yoke – which could not exist if there was not the original archetypal mind. For anything physical to exist, there must first be the archetypal "everything" through which anything can become manifest into a physical experience. The yoke binds the mind to the physical and is housed within the embodiment of a physical body. Embodiment is the ninth concept; the ninth number; an odd number; the second archetype of the body; masculine by number, but the yin to the Yoke's yang; the physical form of the formless.

...

Secrets

Of The Body
Ancient Hebrew – "Yud"
...

10. Right Hand

Part 1 | Pillars

3. Right Hand

The right hand in the majority of humans is demonstrated to be the hand of strength – the hand of action. The archetype of the right hand should be meditated upon in both the physical and metaphorical contexts. The right hand is symbolic of having something to give, hence old adages such as "I would give my right arm for _____." The right arm is the very definition of abundance manifested into the physical. If a person has a hand to lend, it exemplifies abundance. The right hand is the tenth concept; the tenth number; an even number; the third archetype of the body; feminine by number, but yang in the context of the Body; it represents the physical form through which a measurement of excess is defined.

...

Secrets

Of The Body
Ancient Hebrew – "Kaph"

...

11. Humbled Receiver

Part 1 | Pillars

4. Humbled Receiver

The humbled receiver is a concept that cannot be defined by a single word in the English language in order to adequately circumscribe the concept. This concept is best illustrated as the one in need and who is willing to accept the anointing by the hand of another. If the right hand is the physical demonstration of the outward expression of abundance, the humbled receiver is the physical demonstration of someone or something in need of receiving this outward expression. If the receiver is not humbled, pure acceptance cannot occur. Thus, the definition of "humbled receiver" must consist of the object of the archetype and a description that illustrates the state of existence of the object. Humbled receiver is the eleventh concept; the eleventh number; an odd number; the fourth archetype of the body; masculine in number, but the yin to the right hand's yang; one that is open to humbly receiving.

...

Secrets

Of The Body
Ancient Hebrew – "Lamed"
...

ل

ﻟ

ﻟ

ﻟ

ﻟ

ל

12. Guide/Shepherd

Part 1 | Pillars

5. Guide/Shepherd

To guide, to shepherd, to tend to a flock, to lead without being the leader – this is the fifth archetype of the Body. The concept must be meditated upon by combining the concepts illustrated above because one visualization alone cannot encompass the overall meaning of this archetype. Much like a shepherd can tend a flock of sheep and help the sheep navigate, he does not have to be the perceived leader to give guidance. He is the unseen force that discreetly nudges the flock as it demonstrates the need for shepherding. Guide is the twelfth concept; the twelfth number; the fifth concept of the Body; feminine in number, but the yang to Reason's yin; an even number; Guide is the outward expression of the capacity to help and aligns with the fifth archetype of the Mind – revelation.

...

Secrets

Of The Body
Ancient Hebrew – "Mem"

...

13. Reason

6. Reason

In water, find reason. The embodiment of water can be seen as the physical representation of knowledge – of all that is. Water in its purest form has absorption qualities unlike no other on Earth. Unlike fire, water follows a logical path of flow. It can be contained, it can be channeled in its flow. Water is the life source of all living things. It gives life, it contains life. If split into its elemental components, it is the air we breathe that allows us to exist. Water expands when frozen, and shrinks when heated, which is unlike any other naturally occurring matter. Though science may not be able to define why water has the properties it does, it must be accepted for what it is. This is tantamount to reason, because just as a person can be guided, the understanding of the guidance is less important as the guidance itself. As water is absorbent, so is reason. Reason is the absorption of guidance and the rationale of why it must be – though it can only be understood for what had been made available, and not through a complete understanding of all that Is. Reason is the sixth archetype of the Body; the thirteenth concept and thirteenth number; an odd number masculine in gender, but the yin to Guide's yang. It is the inward receipt of guidance and aligns with the sixth archetype of the Mind – the nail.

...

Secrets

Of The Body
Ancient Hebrew – "Nun"
...

14. Seed

7. Seed

Like the seventh archetype of the Mind, the seventh archetype of the Body should be seen as a method to do work – to create motion through the preceding six archetypes of the Body. A seed is a vehicle through which life is given. When a seed is planted, life springs forth. Some seeds can be left untended and still take root. Other seeds need careful care and attention in order for the life to sprout and survive. During the early stages of growth, special attention is needed to ensure the roots are strong enough to allow the life that sprouted forth from the seed to become self-sustaining. The seed is iconic in the representation of the means through which any thought, emotion or guidance can be delivered. The seed is the seventh archetype of the Body; the fourteenth concept; the fourteenth number, an even number; feminine in gender making the seven archetypes of the body feminine in overall existence.

...

Of The Spirit

The words of the Spirit should be thought of as a division of the Mind that serves both as an identity and as a conduit for the Mind. The Body houses the Spirit. So while the Body is subservient to the Mind, the Spirit is subservient to the Body in its rooted form. However, it is important to understand that since the Spirit is the vessel through which the Mind is accessible, the Body is also subservient to the greater construct of the Spirit. The Body should be observed as the vessel for experience and the Spirit should be observed as the vessel for the Mind. Thus, both vessels must coexist during the human experience. The Spirit is a melding of yin and yang, but through which yang is the measured dominant leaving the construct of the Spirit to gravitate toward the Masculine – though it does embody both the masculine and the feminine definitions.

...

Secrets

Of The Spirit
Ancient Hebrew – "Samech"
...

15. Prop/Pillar

Part 1 | Pillars

1. *Prop/Pillar*

The Prop/Pillar is the physical representation of strength. But the definitions of each concept of the Spirit should not be observed as physical – only a physical representation of that which cannot be seen. To define the spirit, one must meditate upon what the spirit is in its entirety, with no beginning and no end. The definition of Prop/Pillar is finite in earthly form, but the definition that should be explored is an infinite Prop/Pillar – a support structure that exists everywhere and in everything. The idea of the spirit must be seen as an invisible strength that resides not just within the body, but within all things. It is the first archetype in the third division of archetypes. With the understanding of the eternal existence of the Mind through which forms the body, the Spirit should be seen as the subdivision of the Mind that exists within the body, yet has no defined beginning or end: an infinite spirit of strength within life. Prop/Pillar is the fifteenth number; an odd number; masculine in gender, the yang to Experience's yin.

...

Secrets

Of The Spirit
Ancient Hebrew – "Ayin"
...

16. Experience/Soul

Part 1 | Pillars

2. Experience/Soul

Experience should best be understood as the embodiment of the Prop/Pillar. An embodiment of the Spirit could best be defined as the Soul, but is not limited to the Soul as defined with the limitations of the human connection to the body. The soul is the embodiment of how a division of the Mind is able to experience everything that Is. The word Experience should not be limited in definition to the action of feeling/seeing/hearing/etc., but rather the understanding of an observable portion of All That Is that, for at least a portion of time, has a defined embodiment, and is what a human would identify as his soul; his essence. But the spirit experience is not limited to just the embodiment of the Body, because the spirit is like a river flowing through everything that is. Therefore, Experience is defined as the observance of all that occurs through the embodiment of the Body, not limited to the constraints of observable earthly time through sight. Experience is the second archetype of the Spirit; the sixteenth overall archetype; the number sixteen; an even number, feminine in gender; the yin to Prop/Pillar's yang – which could not exist in understanding without the other being present. Experience is analogous to the Mind's second archetype: the house, and the Body's second archetype: embodiment.

...

Secrets

Of The Spirit
Ancient Hebrew – "Pey"

...

17. Wisdom/Passion

Part 1 | Pillars

3. Wisdom/Passion

Like the third archetype of the Mind and the Body, the third archetype of the Spirit is the definition of abundance in a spiritual sense. When one has attained knowledge and understanding that overflows in immeasurable quantity, the definition of Wisdom/Passion is assigned. Wisdom/Passion is different than a person being smart or knowledgeable, for wisdom is the definition of a quantity of knowledge and understanding that is in abundance, often manifested in the earthly walk through the Word and through breath. Passion is the outward expression of spiritual abundance. Wisdom is an overflow – a wealth of knowledge and understanding. It is the breath expounded as unto passion. There is not a word that wraps these two words together adequately, but they should be seen as one. The combination of these two words helps to separate this archetype from the common definitions of being smart or knowledgeable. The definition of being smart or knowledgeable of a certain topic should, instead, best be understood as "par for the course, but with potential to improve and refine." Wisdom/Passion is the third archetype of the spirit; the seventeenth concept; the seventeenth number, masculine in gender; the yang to desire's yin.

...

Secrets

Of The Spirit
Ancient Hebrew – "Tsade"
...

18. Desire

4. Desire

As Wisdom/Passion is the representation of abundance of the Spirit, Desire is the representation of the thirst for Wisdom/Passion. Desire is a call to passion, an inner tug at the soul to be fulfilled. Desire is not lust, for lust involves earthly constructs. Desire is the inner voice of the Spirit calling out for fulfillment. Think of how opposite-poled magnets are attracted to each other. This is how desire should be observed; a force of attraction to that which has abundance. Desire is subservient to Wisdom/Passion, but one cannot exist in definition without the other, for there must be Desire for Wisdom/Passion to have a point of measurement – though the measurement should always be understood to be relative, not absolute. Desire is the eighteenth archetype; the fourth archetype of the Spirit; the eighteenth number, feminine in gender; the yin to Wisdom/Passion's yang. Desire is tantamount to the fourth archetype of the Mind – potential, and the fourth archetype of the Body – humbled receiver.

...

Secrets

Of The Spirit
Ancient Hebrew – "Quph"
...

19. Help/Faith

5. Help/Faith

Help/Faith is the Spiritual embodiment of the vehicle for the preceding four archetypes. Help/Faith is a concept whereby the spirit pushes through the physical body to those in need. Often faith is misinterpreted as hope, but faith is an action – an embodiment of the demonstration of the spirit; a divine revelation. Help/Faith is not limited to physical action, but also action through knowledge and harmony. Often, a person desires to help someone because they are in need of something that the spirit can help fulfill. It is the motion of the magnetic attraction of Wisdom/Passion and Desire. It is a calling within to assist another – to bring harmony unto another spirit. Help/Faith is the nineteenth archetype; the fifth archetype of the Spirit; the nineteenth number, masculine in gender; the yang to Attain/Hope's yin. Help/Faith is tantamount to the fifth archetypes of the Mind and the Body, which are Revelation & Guide respectively.

...

Secrets

Of The Spirit
Ancient Hebrew – "Resh"

...

20. Attain/Hope

6. Attain/Hope

Attainment is a concept through which the receipt of Help/Faith is produced. To attain is not to be seen as the definition of self achievement, but rather, the Spiritual reaching of new heights. Attain by modern definition lacks the scope of the definition that is truly conveyed through the archetype, that is why it is coupled with the word Hope. For, hope is the method of holding onto faith. And faith cannot be held without hope. This archetype represents the landscape of the potential of anything achievable through the spirit, but is not embodied through the identity of self. Attainment is something that can manifest through All That Is. Attain/Hope is the sixth archetype of the Spirit and should be seen as reaching a metaphorical summit of an ever increasing higher plateau for spiritual growth, wherein each summit is just a point of measurement for the upward journey. Attain/Hope is the twentieth archetype, the twentieth number, feminine in gender, the yin to Help/Faith's yang. It is tantamount to the sixth archetypes of the Mind and Body: Nail and Reason respectively.

...

Secrets

Of The Spirit
Ancient Hebrew – "Shin"

...

Ш

ς

w

w

ע

שׁ

21. Radiate/Love

7. Radiate/Love

The seventh archetype of the spirit is also not clearly articulated through a single word in modern translation. To radiate is to shine, to grow, to blossom, to glow. If the seventh archetype of the Mind is Plow wherein the motion of the preceding six archetypes of the Mind are put into motion, and the seventh archetype of the Body is Seed, wherein the motion of the preceding six archetypes of the Body are put into motion, to Radiate/Love is the motion of the preceding six archetypes of the Spirit. Radiate can be symbolized through fire and teeth (think about how a smile radiates positive energy and how a snarl radiates negative energy). Radiate is the demonstration of the Spirit in motion. It is Love – a spiritual Love not of direct earthly connotation. As the ground must be plowed for a seed to be planted, the seed must receive some sort of radiation to sprout forth. The energy the seed receives can be understood as the sun's radiation. But the seed also blossoms, which can be seen as the outward radiant expression of the radiation received from the sun. Radiate/Love is the seventh archetype of the Spirit; the twenty-first overall archetype; the twenty-first number, masculine in gender making the Spirit overall masculine in overall existence. Ego's surrender to the first twenty-one archetypes results in the Spirit shining through the Mind and Body planting seeds and giving life to All That

Secrets

Is while simultaneously thirsting for even greater spiritual radiation. Above all, it is the truest definition of the outward expression of Love.

...

Of Unity & Choice

The words of the first twenty-one archetypes have illustrated the motion of thought through the mind, body, and spirit. These pillars are broken into three distinct divisions so that each person can learn to identify the distinction of the trinity of the Mind, Body, and Spirit within. A person can fully embrace all that has been taught through the first twenty-one pillars without ever fully understanding the twenty-second pillar. But, to do so, would be akin to driving blindly through the darkness. The twenty-second pillar is the definition of choice, unity, and freewill. This is where the acceptance or denial of surrendering everything to Christ occurs. This pillar holds greater meaning than all of the other pillars, for it is the definition of completion. Understanding the twenty-second pillar is the most important and intricate aspect of spiritual growth through the progression of the pillars, but it cannot occur without a person first manifesting the first twenty-one pillars into being. This is also the original intention behind the ancient definition of PI (22/7 or, in modern terms, 3.14). It is the completion of a circle where the whole will always be greater than the sum of the parts.

...

Secrets

Of Unity & Choice
Ancient Hebrew – "Tav"
...

22. Divinity/The Arc

Part 1 | Pillars

∞ *Divinity/The Arc* ∞

The twenty-second archetypal concept is Divinity/the Arc. This concept is the final step in the archetypal progression to understanding the human experience. Through the understanding of the seven archetypes of the Mind, the seven archetypes of the Body, and the seven archetypes of the Spirit, a choice remains to be made as to whether to accept all that which has been learned, or to not accept the Spirit. This archetype carries both the same connotation as "freewill" as well as acceptance of enlightenment. When Divinity/the Arc is observed as "the Arc" alone, it is the quintessential definition of the union of the mind, body, and spirit. Once the mind, body, and spirit grow throughout the progression of the 22 archetypes, a spiritual Love is understood in a way that cannot be understood by earthly means alone. The only concept that can transcend time and space is Love. Love is an arc created between Heaven and Earth through the unity of the Mind, Body and the Spirit. And like unto how an arc connects two points in a brilliant flash of light and energy, the arc should also be observed in modern context as well. Noah's Ark was a vessel between two points in time – the end of the Earth that was, and the beginning of God's new creation. The Ark of the Covenant was the vessel through which the Spirit transcended the Heavens and manifested spiritual action on Earth. An arc of

Secrets

energy is tantamount to the modern interpretation of an ark as a great vessel when understood in its most archetypal form. It is the twenty-second number, feminine as defined by number, through which acceptance of the archetype denotes subservience to The Almighty, but balances the yins and the yangs which connote unity to All That Is. The twenty-second archetype is to be understood as the next sequential archetype in the series and the first archetype of the next phase of spirituality. Divinity/The Arc is the bookend to Strength. So if strength is defined as All That Was and All That Is, divinity/the arc must represent All That Will Be in unity. Pictorially, the twenty-second archetype originated in form as a cross, but later transcended into the same shape used to represent the number PI. Ancient PI was defined as 22/7 for it was based on the twenty-two archetypes comprised of three groups of seven. There is no more definition that can exist, and no more understanding that can be gleaned, for it is the final archetype of the human experience and the beginning of the next experience.

...

PART 2

Foundation Stones

Introduction to Foundation Stones

The first part of this Book, Secrets, introduces the concepts of words in motion: pillars to understanding. These words in motion are the most fundamental archetypes of the human experience. There is a special progression through each archetype to which a person must humble himself to proceed to the next archetype of understanding. It is not as simple as understanding an archetype such as "abundance" and knowing how a person should provide abundance to someone in need. It is the embodiment of each archetype and the refinement of the soul to wholly demonstrate the archetype at the soul's most primal level that enables a person's second birth: the birth of their being into their soul. It is also important to understand that for the rebirth to take place, each person must always begin at the beginning: Strength.

To understand communication through archetypes is to understand how souls converse and how the Great Spirit speaks through All That Is. Understanding the archetypes opens the eyes to all of the symbolism packed within a simple moment, a simple gesture. And while it may take a while for

Secrets

students of this knowledge to begin to understand the communication already taking place to them through nature, through circumstances, and through the people and words that surround them, once the archetypes are embraced and the bounds of the Ego released, the conversation God has been trying to have with you all along is revealed.

Mankind communicates through words, through language. These are the constructs that help mankind illustrate thought from one person to the next. But just as the archetypes in understanding the Divine language are revealed, the understanding of how language came to be is equally as important. Many people choose to read words linearly. Sometimes, people will see symbolism. Others will see metaphors and parables in the way words are written. But it is most important to understand the words archetypally. This is not the same as seeing symbolism. They may sound the same in principle, but the truth is these approaches could not be any more different. So, as Part 2 of Secrets is revealed, take time to study, to digest the words, and to humble the Ego in seeking wisdom to All That Is. Gaining this wisdom should be seen as a process like earning a degree or building a career – not as studying for a test, even though you may pass the test with flying colors. It is the application of the knowledge, the removal of the Ego, and the humbled embodiment of the soul where growth occurs.

Of the Origin of Language

Through the origin of the 22 archetypal concepts, communication was born. The very first languages held to the constraints of twenty-two character alphabets that mirrored the archetypal meanings, represented by images that called to the recognition of the archetypes. Only through the evolution of language were more characters created in order to better illustrate phonetics (the way a word should sound) or to better illustrate the numeric system. Though modern Hebrew consists of 27 characters (of which the difference is important to understand at another point in time, but for now, just know that modern Hebrew has 22 letters, with 5 letters having dual meanings/usages), it was originally founded upon a 22 character alphabet and existed in that form for thousands of years. Each of the first 21 characters were divided into 3 groups representing the archetypal concepts of the mind, body and spirit. The 22nd character represented the whole, unity, divinity, completion, choice.

Every language brought forth into earthly existence was founded upon these same 22 archetypal concepts. Every letter represented more than just a sound. Each character held a meaning, a position in the alphabet, a numeric value, an iconic visual representation, and a sound that represented the archetype. One could argue that Hebrew is the original language of the Divine, but to do so is to dismiss the greater recognition of existence. The language of the Divine is the communication of the 22 archetypal concepts through any medium of communication. The most ancient languages of our time – whether initially drawing from another language or not – were all created with the same intent: to communicate the language of the Divine through these 22 archetypal concepts.

These archetypes are the very foundation of theological academia as well as the occult – though each side tends to dismiss the other. Even the original tarot found within the pyramids of ancient Egypt was formed from the collection of 22 images that visually represented the same archetypal concepts through motifs with relative meaning during their time. But, over time, the meanings of the archetypes became lost and hidden through phonetics, mysticism and magic. Man's ego found strength in knowledge and, so in, tried to control the exposure to the most foundational elements of existence for fear of losing control of the people. The ego is the root of modern religions, though most every active practitioner recognizes some innate internal truth hidden deep within. It is the same central truth within Buddhism, Hinduism, Islam, Judaism, Kabbalah, and Christianity. In fact, each of the aforementioned religions were initially founded upon these

Part 2 | Foundation Stones

archetypes, though the message has been lost or hidden from the masses over time. Ironically, the heart of the archetypal concepts in modern times is most widely found within the occult, though each group's lens of understanding is very acute though limited in relation to the potentiality of the underlying breadth of knowledge. Typically, the occult embraces the ego, which leads to misrepresentations of these primal concepts.

In understanding the 22 archetypes and the relationships of the three groupings of seven, one now has a foundational knowledge of the origin of all written languages in antiquity. Each archetype was given a symbol to represent the meaning. These symbols (or pictographs as they are called in modern times) are the original "letters" of written language. These archetypal letters could be grouped together to create motion of archetypal concepts. This motion flows from the first concept to the last giving groups of letters more defined meaning. Through the motion of letters, words were born. Words gave way to sentences, sentences to paragraphs, paragraphs to subjects, subjects to books, et cetera. So in understanding each of the 22 concepts discussed in the section entitled *Pillars*, one may now assume an understanding of the 22 letters of the Hebrew alphabet as well as most any other foundational language.

In ancient Hebrew, the first letter of the alphabet, Aleph, means "strength." The second letter, Beyt, means "house." When put together, the letters aleph-beyt are pronounced "ah-buh" – meaning "father" – of which the archetypal meaning is "the strength of the house." Modern pronunciation of Father

Secrets

in Hebrew evolved into "abba" though the origin is still based on the original ancient Hebrew characters: aleph-beyt. In fact, if one were to take each word in ancient Hebrew and write out the archetypal concepts of the letters that form the word, there could be a conclusion drawn to the modern meaning without ever having to know the literal definition of the word in question. The same holds true for other ancient languages such as Arabic, Latin, and Greek. In Hebrew, the first letter of a word carries the greatest foundational meaning. Each additional letter represents a chain of concepts strung together to form a more precise concept. The final character carries with it a meaning of closure or expanse to the concept. Since the original archetypes were ordered by the way in which they came into existence, their representative letters carried archetypal numeric meanings. This means that by stringing together letters, a layer of numeric information is also conveyed on the layers of Mind, Body and Spirit. Words were used interchangeably with numbers, sometimes indicated only by a symbol at the beginning of the word to help a person reading the information know to use the numeric value instead of the word. However, it is important to understand that words were architected to carry specific numeric values that were associated with ancient geometry and the creation of All That Is – so the original number values of words should be seen as equally important as the meaning. The importance of the numeric meaning holds just as much value to those versed in the sacred language of geometry.

Part 2 | Foundation Stones

In the original creation of Divine language, each person was capable of understanding the symbolic, archetypal, literal, and numeric meanings instantly – without additional thought. But in modern times, the human brain has been trained to interpret linearly, without depth. This is why the original writings in literature are the most valuable artifacts of ancient history. They hold within the characters multiple dimensions of understanding. There has always been a fundamental reason why certain books of the Bible, Quran and Apocryphal texts warn the reader that the message can only be conveyed through the original written form – not through translation. This is also one of the reasons why the greatest controlling forces globally have concealed the original texts to the oldest books of time and not provided exposure of them to the masses. If man were to learn that which is being communicated through this text, then the concept of power and order would be lost to the shift of consciousness toward Love and unity that will ultimately, in time, prevail.

So in the evolution of language, one can see how the original pictorial representations of the most ancient alphabets evolved/devolved over time. The first letter in ancient Hebrew was first represented by the image of an oxen's head, a visual representation for the archetype of strength. Eventually the letter devolved into the three lines that comprise the letter, A. The ancient transitional texts appear to demonstrate the devolution of the oxen image into a short-hand version of the oxen's head and horns consisting of three crossing lines that look like a sideways A. In more modern times, the sideways oxen line drawing was eventually turned upright to form the modern letter, A. In the letter's current form, the triangle and crossbar still illustrate the concept of strength through the representation of the strongest structure that can be perfectly created in the human experience. So whether the A was intended to represent a triangle or a shorthand version of an oxen's head and horns, it is important to observe that nature demonstrated the keys to the divine knowledge before man understood nature's way of communication.

If one desires to better understand the aforementioned evolution of language and how it ties to the archetypal Divine, the most obvious Hebrew character to study both the visual and aural meaning is the fifth letter of the Hebrew alphabet. This letter is pronounced "Hey" and has managed to withstand the deterioration of the archetypal concepts over the course of the formation of new languages. As discussed earlier, the fifth character carries the archetypal meaning of "revelation." Unsurprisingly, the original pictograph form of the letter is a stick figure with both hands raised up on either side of the stick figure's head. The image evokes the concept of a great reveal or surprise. In modern times, one of the most basic things a person can do in order to call out for attention to another is to raise a hand out and exclaim "Hey!" It is no coincidence that "revelation" is the fifth archetypal concept and is represented by the number five, for the number five is embodied through the five fingers of the outstretched hand. In modern English, the character for the Hebrew letter "hey" is H – which is still representative of the devolution of the origi-

Part 2 | Foundation Stones

nal stick drawing. The modern H has omitted the circle that would have represented the person's head. If it were not for that omission, the H could be viewed as arms raised and legs below. Perhaps the grandest gesture of all for man to rediscover in the Divine architecture of language, is that the most "revealing" letter of this ancient truth is illustrated through the letter carrying the archetypal meaning of "revelation" thus demonstrating how everything is connected – regardless of how disjointed it may at first appear.

Though the origin of language is what has been discussed in this section, the same archetypal concepts permeate nature, the anatomy, and the cosmos. It is important to remember these concepts are archetypal by definition – and archetypal means the very foundation of All That Is. These same core archetypes can be found in music, art, math, science, biology, philosophy, theology and geometry.

Of The Seven Loci

The human experience begs for the answers to questions that formulate a complete understanding of a particular concept. The questions that are posed as the means by which complete understanding of a concept can be defined are traditionally known as the five W's: who, what, when, where, why. Additionally a sixth question is recognized to help form a better understanding of the overall concept. This question is "how." But, "how" is an inadequate question to ask because the answer is already covered by the definition found in the first three W's: who, what, and when. The need for an additional sixth question to supplement the 5 W's demonstrates a void existing in the 5 W's that would help a person reach the complete understanding of a concept. This void should actually be defined by two questions: "in what way?" and "by what means?" Ancient Greek philosophy acknowledged this principle of understanding as a concept called "the seven circumstances" – known in Latin as "Quis, quid, quando, ubi, cur, quem ad modum, quibus adminiculis." This phrase translates into "who, what, when, where, why, in what way, by what means."

Secrets

Whether the parallels of the "seven circumstances" to the original 22 archetypes and their respective subdivisions had already been drawn at that time in history is not readily apparent. But in this present moment it is important to realize that the seven loci required to fully understand any archetypal concept are the very loci that comprise the motion of the archetypes within the three tenets (mind, body and soul) – for each of the three divisions of the Hebrew alphabet consist of seven archetypes each. These archetypes align perfectly with the seven loci as originally defined in Greek philosophy and answer the questions as to why the archetypes must exist in their original form. To see how the loci parallel with the Mind, the loci/archetype pairings would occur as follows: (1) strength = who, (2) house = what, (3) abundance = when, (4) potential = where, (5) revelation = how, (6) nail = by what means, and (7) plow = in what way. To place the loci into the motion of comprehension would be to illustrate the seven archetypes of the mind by saying the following: "Who is the mind? The strength – All That Is. What defines the strength? The house, or container in which it is held. When is the strength to act or do something? When there is an abundance relative to another's potential. Where will the action take place? In the location of potential. Why will this action occur? Because there is an outward expression of abundance and it must be revealed/expressed in a location of potential. The answer to why is the defined concept of revelation. In what way will the abundance be delivered? Through the inward receipt of the

Part 2 | Foundation Stones

outward expression (a nail). By what means will the abundance be delivered? Through the motion analogous to the plow."

When applied to the Body, the following pairs are created: (1) yoke=who, (2) embodiment=what, (3) right hand=when, (4) humbled receiver=where, (5) to guide=why, (6) reason=by what means, (7) seed=in what way. To place the loci into motion for the concept of the body would be to illustrate the seven archetypes by asking these questions: "Who is the body? The yoke that binds the mind and soul. What is the body? The embodiment of the mind. When is the body to act or do something? When there is a abundance of anything to give – metaphorically represented by "lending a hand." Where will this action take place? In a location humbled to receive. Why will this action occur? Because there is a person/location in humbled need of a helping hand, so the hand shall serve as a shepherd – to guide, to prod, to lead. This is the concept of teacher and student: teach/learn and learn/teach. In what way will guidance occur? Through reason. By what means will the guidance of the abundance be delivered? By placing a seed (as a gardener would do)."

Finally, when these concepts are applied to the Spirit, the archetype/loci pairings are as follows: (1) prop/pillar = who, (2) experience = what, (3) wisdom/passion = when, (4) desire=where, (5) help/faith = why, (6) attainment of heights/hope = in what way, (7) radiance/Love = by what means. When posed into motion, the loci/archetype pairings are illustrated as follows: "Who is the spirit? The prop/pillar of the body and the mind. What is the spirit? The experiencer of everything – experienced through the body and interpreted by the mind – the embodiment of the soul. When is the spirit to act or do something? When wisdom/passion exists – an overflow of the soul. Where will the action take place? In the location of desire. Why will the action take place? Because a person desiring wisdom/passion is in need of help/faith. In what way will wisdom/passion occur? Through the attainment of greater spiritual heights, better known as hope. By what means will wisdom/passion be delivered? By spiritual radiance/Love – shining moments that cause spiritual recognition in another to occur. This is the outward expression of faith through spirituality."

And though the seven loci do not apply directly to the 22nd archetype, they indirectly form an equation for the human experience: when each of the three groups of the seven archetypes and loci have been fully understood and embraced in their purest capacity, enlightenment can be attained. This is a conscious choice – a sum that is greater than all of the parts combined, but dependent on complete acceptance of each part in their respective entirety in order to form the foundation. The experiencer may accept the first 21 archetypes, but the 22nd is represented by choice/divinity/the arc – better known as free will. This is the decision that must be made to accept or deny all that has been learned. The 22nd archetype should be observed as the arc created when the three tenets of seven find unity – like unto an electrical arc of energy created between two points.

Of Thy Self

There comes a time during the journey of the human experience that consciousness can become independently acknowledged in the brain. This is quite possibly better defined as the awareness that consciousness exists in a greater capacity than the mind alone, the spirit alone, or the body alone. When that recognition occurs, it is likely that the human brain will seek to identify it's consciousness's identity. The mind's attempt at seeking identity would be equivalent to the concept of a person with amnesia seeking to learn his name. However, the question of "who" is a paradox – for consciousness cannot be identified by asking "who." If consciousness could be identified by who, it would be identified as the sum of All that Is, the yoke of the mind, body and spirit, and the prop represented as the soul (each of the "who" loci). This in and of itself, is the definition of the identity of God in a form independent from the understanding of God as All that Is. But – "what" consciousness is can be identified because it is the sum of the yin to the yang. Consciousness could not exist without the existence of the strength, the yoke and the soul. Therefore, consciousness is the sum of the house, the embodiment, and the experience. The identity of each unique consciousness is the motion – the flux-like state of the experience. "Who am I" is not a question that has an answer. However, by asking "what am I?" the experiencer demonstrates a humbled recognition in consciousness's identity as subservient to All that Is in the Kingdom of God.

PART 3

Song of the Spheres

Introduction to Song of the Spheres

Oh, song oh, song of the spheres, your essence is the very foundation of All That Is, All That Was and All That Will Be. The sweet song of Your surrender leaves a resonance rippling through the aether, wafting through the eternal drift from one tangent to the next on the quest to find Destiny's calling. The sonnet of Your words leaves an indelible mark upon existence and the Spiritual remembrance from whence we were once birthed into Your very presence. Oh, holy art Thou in divine splendor and perfect design, a masterful architecture of unblemished perfection; direction conceived on the arc of aetheric curves winding, twisting, spiraling throughout the great expanse of All. Humbled be they who desire to walk in the path of understanding and righteousness, whom long to quench their thirst in the wellspring of equidistant knowledge that blossoms forth from the perfection of the Divine beauty of Heaven's omnipresent yore. Blessed, oh, Creator of All who has chosen to allow these words to be henceforth spoken.

Of The Sphere

The concept of infinity having no beginning and no end is one of the most difficult concepts for the human mind to understand. However, the idea can be more easily comprehended by first backing into a three-dimensional idea of a construct and then removing the boundaries. So let us begin. First, imagine a circle. If it helps, visualize a circle drawn on a piece of paper. The circle is the very definition of two-dimensional equidistance – no beginning and no end. Every place on the circle's diameter measures exactly the same as the point directly across from it. Now imagine the circle is a three-dimensional sphere. The drawing on the paper will not change. The mind has just added imaginary depth to the circle. Again, every point contains the same equidistance as any other point along the boundary – except this time there is a third dimension that adheres to the same principles of the two-dimensional circle. Now imagine expanding the sphere so that all sides of the sphere are now outside the boundary of the paper. The paper will appear blank, but is actually a small window peering into a portion of the sphere. This is how humans define time: a window into a portion of All That Is.

Secrets

The sphere is the most perfect definition of equidistance – no beginning and no end. Because a sphere is perfect in form, it does not contain any straight edges and therefore cannot have any "points" defined, for a point is defined as the intersection of two joining edges. Since a sphere does not contain any straight edges, it must be the most perfect example of equidistance that could exist in the Mind's eye. But, even if for a moment, a sphere is defined with size constraints, it is important to understand that any vector passing through any chosen location on the sphere (which will occur on the perpendicular axis to the tangential plane) will always measure the same length regardless of where the point is chosen along the sphere's boundary. In simple terms, this is the definition of the diameter of the sphere – and it can only be defined because the sphere is perfect in design.

So, in understanding that a sphere is the most perfect multi-dimensional concept that the human mind can visualize, it only makes sense that the definition of All That Is must be based on perfect design – not limited to the concept of a sphere, but instead, based on the concept of the sphere at its very foundation. The moment an angle is introduced into the concept of All That Is, a limitation has been defined because an angle can only exist in finite space. This means that the observance of a straight edge or a joint in any medium indicates limitations. The definition of an observed edge can only occur through a limited scope of understanding. There are no other ways around this fact. At one time, modern civilization argued the world was flat because the horizon was all that could be

Part 3 | Song of the Spheres

observed and understood. However, ancient civilizations that predated the "more advanced modern civilization" already understood the concept of the sphere and postulated about the rotation of the planets and stars. There are some that have argued that technology did not exist for ancient civilizations to know about planets and stars or the orbit of the Earth and moon around the sun. But, if one is to only think in concepts of spheres and circles, the observance of everything in the human experience takes on a new light – much easier to discern and understand, but in contradiction to the finite concepts instilled in the mind of modern man. The concept of infinity was long understood by the ancients yet lost in pre-modern times, only to be re-discovered through proofs, science, math and reason.

The definition of an infinite medium being the basis of All That Is does not contradict modern scientific ideas that the universe is constantly expanding, but it would indicate that for the universe to be expanding, there must be an observable wall which would mean that something does not exist outside the boundary of the observable edge. If there truly is an observable end to the universe, this indicates the universe is only a portion of all that is observable in this version of the experience of All That Is and would mean the observable universe cannot be the definition of the container for everything. So in All That Is, All That Was, and All That Will Be, the principle foundation for creation must be based on a sphere – or at least the concepts that the principles of a sphere introduce in divine equidistance. The introduction of any concept outside of per-

Secrets

fect, divine construction introduces flaws into understanding. So, think not of lines, edges and angles, but think only of spheres and circles. This will open the gateway to understanding All That Is.

Of Equidistance

If one were to define infinity and how infinity must be structured, it is first important to understand that infinity is both as infinitely large and as infinitely small as can be conceived – but neither conceivable edge are boundaries because infinity must go on forever. So, what is perceived through the human experience is both equally large in the construct of infinity and equally as small. So while infinity cannot have a line-based structure, it can be structured from infinitely large and small spheres. But how can this be? For it is within these words that the most divine architecture of all shall be revealed.

Imagine a sphere. Now imagine a second sphere of equal size directly behind the first sphere, so that it is unobservable to the human eye. Now imagine a third sphere behind the second sphere, so that three spheres exist where only one is observable in the current field of view. It is important to understand that in the simplest terms, the sphere can represent a simple object that has no motion. In this case, let's say the sphere represents a ball. The first sphere is red, the second yellow, the third is green. To the observer, there is only one ball – and that ball is red based on the observer's viewpoint. From another viewpoint, there are 3 balls. Yet to another observer, there is just one ball – the third, which is green. Though this example is extremely simple, the idea being conveyed is much greater, and is important to understand for the more advanced concepts that will be unveiled.

Now that we have three spheres connected in a line, lets add eight more sets of three so that we have the formation of a cube. This cube is three spheres wide by three spheres tall by three spheres long. Now, for a moment, imagine this is the structure of infinity. If this were the case, it would be a flawed theory because while the spheres represent perfection, and the bundle of spheres represents endless possibilities, the structure created contains space between the spheres due to their perfectly round architecture. This structure is imperfect, though it is based on perfection. In order to make infinity's structure perfect, each sphere must not be understood as solid, but rather as a spherical construct whereby one sphere begins at the very center of the next. Instead of having each sphere rest adjacent to the other, each sphere now starts at the center of the one next to it so that the starting and ending point of each sphere's diameter begins and ends at the center point of the adjacent sphere. In this concept, there are only three axes, because that is the minimum amount of axes required to form infinite bounds with no space between. Thus the Divinity of Three begins to be revealed. Every interconnected sphere now forms the fabric of All That Is without any lines, or any edges. Uniformity of the sphere – regardless of size – creates the same blanketed structure. This is the definition of Divine Equidistance: one perfect shape with no points, regardless of size,

Part 3 | Song of the Spheres

creating a perfect infinity. An infinitely small sphere is the definition of a point. An infinitely large sphere is the definition of All That Is whereby the fabric of All That Is is held together through the equidistant shape of perfection and equidistant balance of polarization of the spheres. Now, imagine the greatest expanse of this fabric compressed down into a single dimension so that the architecture is understood, but the perception is that everything has no definition. This means that every sphere sits exactly on top of the other but has no definition of shape, size, or even existence. This is infinity – infinitely large, infinitely small, infinitely without shape and perceived structure, infinitely with shape and structure – all best understood through the construct of the sphere.

Of The Equidistant Bouquet

Everything that is perceived in the human experience has infinite possibilities of how it can exist, and everything must be interconnected by definition of infinity – though the observance of life in the human experience must be relative in location through infinity's time/space. But what is time? What is space? The easiest way to understand this concept is to view time/space as the vector of perception through the equidistant bouquet. But what is the Equidistant Bouquet? Like a child's pop-up book, the visualization of the Equidistant Bouquet must be understood with similar surprise and awe. Just as the images and words on a page are carefully architected to open up from a two-dimensional plane into a three-dimensional object for a child to observe, the equidistant bouquet must be observed in the same light – with the humility of the eyes and mind of a child.

To understand the Equidistant Bouquet, it is first important to understand the concept of a line. Modern man defines a line as the connection between two points. By this definition, for a line to exist, two points must first exist. A third

Secrets

point is required to create a two-dimensional shape. But the true definition of a line should be understood as the conceptual diameter of a sphere through space. Much has been made in ancient texts of the four corners of the Earth – a concept that has no explanation in current times. But, for a moment, imagine a line. Now, above the line, label it " side A." Below the line, label it " side B." To the left of the line (at its end point) label it " side C" and to the right of the line (at the other end point) label it "side D." Now, imagine that the line is actually a circle turned 90° into three-dimensional space so that only the outermost, infinitely-small arc of the circle is visible in the mind's eye. If the observer was to pull side A toward his viewpoint, and push side B away, the circle would be revealed. The measurement from side C to side D is the diameter, but is also now the same as the measurement from side A to side B. These sides are tantamount to the four corners of the Earth, though by further exploration of this topic, the understanding of how a sphere gains corners will be understood.

With the concept of a line now understood, imagine a perfect square – not a cube, but rather a flat, two-dimensional square. Each one of the connected lines represents a circle turned on its axis so that only the outer edge is observable to the viewer. When this concept is meditated upon, it becomes evident that the definition of a two-dimensional square illustrates the location of a three-dimensional sphere in space. The outline created by the two-dimensional lines is actually a grid that indicates the location of a sphere in space. Now for a moment, imagine the full image of translucent spheres at-

Part 3 | Song of the Spheres

tached along each edge of the cube, instead of the two-dimensional circles that helped envision the shape. The centerline of each sphere will begin and end at the center point of the next. This two-dimensional square has now transformed into a cube, illustrated through eight spheres on each vertex with the ninth sphere located in the very center. This center sphere is the center-point; the sphere which we wanted to identify in the beginning, but had to conceptualize through two-dimensional lines. These nine translucent spheres (currently forming a diamond), when rotated 45° down toward the observer across an imagined three-dimensional axis, appear as seven interlocking spheres – the outlines of which form the basis of the Flower of Life. The mathematical rotation will not produce a perfectly equidistant shape in earthly manifestation, but in equidistance, everything exists in every location simultaneously but must be manifest in perfect equidistance, thus producing the equidistant shape of the seven interlocking spheres. In earthly understanding, this is represented as the three-dimensional model of the Seed of Life, but the three-dimensional model interpretation introduces more confusion as it attempts to quantify infinity through a physical recreation of something that cannot be recreated. The concept of three dimensions should be observed as an illusion rather than something tangible (though understandably it is difficult to observe this concept through an earthly lens of understanding because humans perceive and accept their existence as in three tangible dimensions).

Secrets

With the explanation of the birth of the Flower of Life, the concept of Nine has been introduced – as well as the concept of Seven. Nine gives birth to Seven which holds within it the Seed of Life – one perfect sphere within. This is why the Fabric of All is known as the Equidistant Bouquet, for all life contains within it a seed that sprouts forth into a flower. In order of precedence of divine growth, the bouquet must always contain an incremental prime number of spheres as laid out horizontally and vertically for the illusion of the third dimension to continue to manifest and hold within it the Seed of Life, which within it will hold the Divine Seed. This is the Secret of the Primes. When translucent spheres are aligned in a 3 x 3 x 3 grid and rotated 45° counterclockwise (to form a diamond) and 45° down through an imagined three-dimensional axis, the twenty-seven translucent spheres appear as nineteen visible spheres in the mind's eye (nine are hidden from the observer's view). This is the complete depiction of the Flower of Life. As demonstrated through a two-dimensional drawing of the nineteen interlocking spheres, the Flower of Life holds within it a three-dimensional cube (sometimes called Metatron's cube) that holds within it the Seed of Life, which holds within it the Divine Seed. Both the Flower of Life and the Seed of Life are the geometric methods of creating the hexagon – which is a perfect, six-sided shape that also serves as the elemental structure for carbon: the element required for life to exist as the human experience is to understand it.

As the illusion of geometric shapes is created through the Equidistant Bouquet, it should be understood that this struc-

Part 3 | Song of the Spheres

ture holds true down to the smallest molecular level and all of the way through on the grandest scale. The sheer scale of the expanse of the bouquet illustrates how all things are possible, and how all things are interconnected. The observance of the motion of the objects created should be understood as the occurrence of sequential potentials occurring on a particular vector. At this point, it should now be apparent why it was earlier stated that the perceived third dimension should be viewed as a pop-up book that children read. The third dimension is manifested from an infinitely small, yet infinitely large, Equidistant Bouquet of spheres that are flat when viewed transparently on an axis, yet hide within their construct the dimensional understanding created by the observable spheres as well as the spheres that "disappear" from view. The twist of the axes of the observable structure of the universe should henceforth be understood as circular polarization. Depending on perspective, the polarization is either left-handed polarization or right-handed polarization. It is also important to observe that circular polarization was one of the most revered concepts throughout ancient history of man, though its translation has been lost throughout the modern ages. The scarab beetle is one of the most well known symbols of ancient Egypt but with reasons unknown to modern man until now. The reason of the beetle's significance is the way in which the beetle's shell demonstrates a concept not found anywhere else in land-based nature – the demonstration of circular polarization of light. This polarization gives the scarab beetle's shell the metallic glow and iridescence that can be witnessed by the naked

Secrets

eye. To a person familiar with the concept of the Equidistant Bouquet and the twist of the axes surrounding the vector of time, the scarab beetle represents every divine concept in the understanding of All That Is. There is no other significance as grand as the demonstration of HOW the mechanics of All That Is is manifested in the nature of mankind's surroundings.

 Since the illusion of three-dimensional space is created by the circular-polarized viewpoint of the Equidistant Bouquet, the grid of energy flowing amongst the spheres must also follow a geometric pattern to manifest the illusion of three-dimensional space in place. As illustrated before, the Flower of Life is created through the polarized twist of a 3 x 3 x 3 grid of equidistant spheres creating 19 observable spherical boundaries. The three-dimensional cube is the space in which the Seed of Life and Divine Seed reside. But through the polarized twist of perspective to the Equidistant Bouquet, the polarized energy of the spheres must adhere to a specific geometric pattern – which is also based on the Principal of Five. In this case, a pentagon is the perfect geometric formation of five lines. In three-dimensional space, when all five sides of the pentagon are attached in a soccer-ball like fashion, the shape of a dodecahedron is created. This is the last solid identified by Plato, and is also in the background of Salvador Dali's painting of The Last Supper. The dodecahedron consists of Twelve pentagonal faces, consisting of twenty vertices and thirty edges. Within the dodecahedron, five separate, perfect cubes can be formed by connecting eight of the twenty vertices. The vertices of the dodecahedron should be observed as the shape pro-

Part 3 | Song of the Spheres

duced by the rotating cube of the Flower of Life. The surrounding dodecahedron of Metatron's cube is the energy and lensing pattern of polarized energy flowing around the Flower of Life and should also be visualized in the same spherical manner used to describe the Flower of Life, the Seed of Life, and Divine Seed. This dodecahedron shall henceforth be called the Basket of Life.

The Basket of Life contains special properties that should be observed and meditated upon. Within the pentagon, a perfect, five-sided star (a pentagram) can be formed by visualizing lines connecting each of the opposite vertices of the pentagram. So, if the three-dimensional visualization of the pentagram is the dodecahedron, the three-dimensional visualization of the dodecahedron with inscribed stars on each pentagram is an icosahedron. The icosahedron contains twenty equilateral triangular faces consisting of thirty edges and twelve vertices – the inverse of the dodecahedron. And, within each star created in the icosahedron, a smaller pentagram is formed. Within this pentagram, another star can be formed. This pattern continues infinitely and is best described in human terms as a fractal. The icosahedron combined with the dodecahedron form the complete energy grid called the Basket of Life that circumscribes and holds the Flower of Life in place. But, think not in terms of lines – only in terms of diameters for translucent spheres that are interconnected. These are the shapes that form all that is observable and able to be experienced through the lens of the human experience.

Of Divine Ratios & Proportions

Divine Ratios and Proportions are used to understand how the perceived material existence of the human experience came to be and was birthed from All That Is producing the manifestation of the illusionary third-dimension through the Equidistant Bouquet. In order to understand that which is experienced, one must first learn all that can be understood from whence the experience was formed. Only through understanding of Divine Equidistance and the twist of perspective into the Equidistant Bouquet can one begin to see how the manifestation of the human experience should be observed as a compressed subset of All That Is (Nine into Seven, Twenty-Five into Nineteen) whereby the illusion expands into three dimensions. This is the explanation of how compression produces the expansion known as the human experience.

In the human experience, mathematics is centered around base-10, which means that numbers are ordered in groups of Ten. In the concept of Divine Equidistance, the illusion of the third dimension is manifested on a Five by Five grid of spheres that create the Flower of Life. But to measure Five spheres in a single direction, there must be Ten defined points since the spheres overlap from one center point to the next – thus demonstrating how base-10 came to be. In base-10, the principle is that Ten discreet points create a group of numbers. But instead of thinking in terms of quantifiable numbers, think in terms of "points" that are tantamount to vertices of a geometric shape. Ten equally spaced points create Nine whole divisions that, in turn, define Five spheres of the Equidistant Bouquet on one illusionary axis. Numbers are nothing more than indicators of points in space that define diameters of spheres. So in terms of equal divisions in base-10, there will always be Nine whole parts.

In terms of Divine Ratios and Proportions, Ten cannot be used as a base for ratios and proportions because Ten is based on finite constructs. Instead, Divine numbers must be formed through the use of base-9, though based on the perception of 10 points. These Nine numbers serve to indicate the whole parts of equal division and not the points – for creation is formed on perfect spheres and not on the illusion of lines and points. Within the human experience, Divine ratios and proportions must be observed relative to the Equidistant Bouquet. Since the Equidistant Bouquet has formed the human experience through the illusion of a three-dimensional cube construct, the group of numbers that form the basis of Divine Ratios and Proportions must be, in effect, three-dimensional. In essence, the numbers must consist of Three digits to adhere to the three-dimensional construct of the cube created within the Flower of Life.

Part 3 | Song of the Spheres

The numbers used to define Divine ratios and proportions are grouped into Nine bundles of Nine number groups consisting of Three units per Side. There are Three sides in totality – a Trinity. In order to understand the mechanics of the Great Ethereal Machine, each number should be understood not to represent a number as known within base-10, but rather a group of Three units that will always reduce-sum in base-9 to Three, Six or Nine. Zero will not appear in these groups, though it can be used as a placeholder outside of the Three Sides of Nine bundles.

The first bundle of Nine number groups should be observed as the example of perfect Divine symmetry and proportion unto earthly understanding. Beginning with the number 111, the numbers should be incremented by one unit per placeholder until a ceiling of 999 is reached. The distance between 111 and 999 should be viewed as the Nine even divisions of the first group of the First Side. This group henceforth shall be known as "The Divine Scale." This first group consists of the number groups 111, 222, 333, 444, 555, 666, 777, 888, and 999. As is evidenced in this bundle, the first number group's sum is Three. The second is Six. The third group is Nine. The fourth group is where base-9 math is put to use. 4 plus 4 equals 8. 8 plus 4 equals 12 – but because 12 is greater than 9, it must be reduced. In this case 1 plus 2 equals Three. The fifth group's sum is Six. The sixth group's sum is Nine. The seventh group's sum is Three. The eighth group's sum is Six. The ninth group's sum is Nine.

Secrets

If the first group of Nine numbers is to be envisioned vertically stacked, the second group of Nine should be viewed as stacked vertically in the same 9 positions, but adjacent to the right of the first bundle of number groups. This second group should have each number group incremented from its horizontal number group neighbor by 12 units (2 plus 1 equals Three). This will produce the series of numbers 123, 234, 345, 456, 567, 678, 789, 891, and 912. The first number group's sum is Six. The second number group's sum is Nine. The third group's sum is Three. The fourth group's sum is Six. The fifth group's sum is Nine. The sixth group's sum is Three. The seventh group's sum is Six. The eighth group's sum is Nine. The ninth group's sum is Three. But, it is important to observe that the numerical distance between 891 and 912 is no longer 111 numerically as perceived within the human experience. The distance is only 11 numerical units (111 base 9 units). This is the beginning of the evidence of the ratcheting mechanism inherent in the Great Ethereal Machine that manifests the circular polarization which is observed through the human experience.

The third bundle of Nine number groups should be vertically stacked and horizontally placed to the right of the second bundle. The same pattern from the second bundle continues by increments of 12 units horizontally (or 111 vertically now that the pattern has manifested). The third bundle produces the following number groups: 135, 246, 357, 468, 579, 681, 792, 813, and 924. The first number group's sum is Nine. The second group's sum is Three. The third group's sum is Six.

Part 3 | Song of the Spheres

The fourth group's sum is Nine. The fifth group's sum is Three. The sixth group's sum is Six. The seventh group's sum is Nine. The eighth group's sum is Three. The ninth group's sum is Six. Again, the ratcheting mechanism of the Great Ethereal Machine is evidenced earlier in the sequence starting one position earlier, between 792 and 813. Additionally, a new pattern emerges horizontally. In the first bundle, the first number group adds to Three. In the second bundle, the first number group adds to Six. In the third bundle, the first number group adds to Nine. So the horizontal pattern of Three, Six and Nine emerges from the bundles. In the same way as the spheres require Three to demonstrate Divine Equidistance, it takes Three bundles of numbers to demonstrate Divine Equidistance in ratios and proportion.

While the following portions of numbers may be laborious to read, it is necessary to include the complete sequence of numbers for clarity and precision of The Divine Word. In order to complete the sequence of the First Side, the fourth bundle of number groups are 147, 258, 369, 471, 582, 693, 714, 825, and 936. The fifth bundle includes these number groups: 159, 261, 372, 483, 594, 615, 726, 837, and 948. The sixth bundle includes the number groups: 162, 273, 384, 495, 516, 627, 738, 849, 951. The seventh bundle includes the number groups: 174, 285, 396, 417, 528, 639, 741, 852, and 963. The eighth bundle includes the number groups: 186, 297, 318, 429, 531, 642, 753, 864, and 975. The ninth bundle includes these number groups: 198, 219, 321, 432, 543, 654, 765, 876, and 987. These Nine number groups comprise the

Secrets

First Side which shall henceforth be known as the Side of Nine and be used to understand the physics and math of the human experience.

The Second Side consists of Nine bundles that increase in increments relative to the bundle positions of the Side of Nine by Six units. The starting point in the first bundle begins at 111 plus 6 which equals 117. The first bundle includes the number groups 117, 228, 339, 441, 552, 663, 774, 885, and 996. The second bundle includes the number groups 129, 231, 342, 453, 564, 675, 786, 897, and 918. The third bundle includes the number groups 132, 243, 354, 465, 576, 687, 798, 819, and 921. The fourth bundle includes the number groups 144, 255, 366, 477, 588, 699, 711, 822, and 933. The fifth bundle includes the number groups 156, 267, 378, 489, 591, 612, 723, 834, and 945. The sixth bundle includes the number groups 168, 279, 381, 492, 513, 624, 735, 846, and 957. The seventh bundle includes the number groups 171, 282, 393, 414, 525, 636, 747, 858, and 969. The eighth bundle includes the number groups 183, 294, 315, 426, 537, 648, 759, 861, and 972. The ninth bundle includes the number groups 195, 216, 327, 438, 549, 651, 762, 873, and 984. The first, fourth, and seventh bundles each have Nine as the sum. The second, fifth, and eighth bundles each add to Three. The third, sixth, and ninth bundles sum to Six. These Nine number groups comprise the Second Side, which shall henceforth be known as the Side of Six.

The Third Side consists of Nine bundles that are increased relative to the bundle positions of the Side of Nine by

Part 3 | Song of the Spheres

Three units. The starting point in the first bundle begins at 111 plus 3 which equals 114. The first bundle includes the number groups 114, 225, 336, 447, 558, 669, 771, 882, and 993. The second bundle includes the number groups 126, 237, 348, 459, 561, 672, 783, 894, and 915. The third bundle includes the number groups 138, 249, 351, 462, 573, 684, 795, 816, and 927. The fourth bundle includes the number groups 141, 252, 363, 474, 585, 696, 717, 828, and 939. The fifth bundle include the number groups 153, 264, 375, 486, 597, 618, 729, 831, and 942. The sixth bundle includes the number groups 165, 276, 387, 496, 517, 628, 739, 841, and 952. The seventh bundle includes the number groups 177, 288, 399, 411, 522, 633, 744, 855, and 966. The eighth bundle includes the number groups 189, 291, 312, 423, 534, 645, 756, 867, and 978. The ninth bundle includes the number groups 192, 213, 324, 435, 546, 657, 768, 879, and 981. The first, fourth, and seventh bundles each total Six. The second, fifth, and eighth bundles each add to Nine. The third, sixth, and ninth bundles each have Three as the sum. These Nine number groups comprise the Third Side which shall henceforth be known as the Side of Three.

While the divisions of the Sides are divided into Nine by Nine grids, the pattern can continue both horizontally and vertically into each sequential fractal by using a zero as a holding place. As an example, the preceding vertical bundle of number groups for the first bundle of the Side of Nine would only contain the numbers 009 and 099 in positions one and nine respectively. The second bundle will contain only the

Secrets

number 012 in position two. The third bundle will contain the number 023 in the third position and so on. The first bundle is much harder to comprehend through words, but the pattern will reveal itself as the numbers are envisioned within a grid. But, the fractal beginning above 999 is much easier to visualize. The first "step into" the fractal occurs at 1011 (111 units above 999, but the left-most unit has moved into the next number in a holding-place sequence, which is 10). The rest of the sequence progressing into the adjacent fractals would appear as: 1011, 1122, 1233, 1344, 1455, 1566, 1677, 1788, 1899, 1911, 2022, 2133, 2244, etc.

Of Seven & The Hidden Within The Nine

The spheres hold within them great mysteries to man while also serving as a gateway into and out of observable time/space as perceived within the human experience. The secret of Nine cannot be easily observed, though the concept of Seven is much more apparent in the human experience. From the dawn of man, the observance of scales in music and the visible light spectrum have been divided into Seven evenly spaced steps consisting of Twelve divisions. The thirteenth division or eighth even step will ascend the pattern into the next octave (or fractal). It is important to observe that a geometric cube has Twelve edges formed by Nine spheres (for further explanation, see the chapter, "Of the Eight-Sphere Cube") which appear as the Seven visible circles in the Seed of Life. This pattern will repeat in concept and construct throughout the understanding of All That Is and the Equidistant Bouquet.

Secrets

But to understand Seven and the mystery of The Hidden within the octave, it is important to understand the concept of Nine. Mankind has already observed and quantified the ratios of Three, Six and Nine within mathematics. One of the most widely known principles in geometry helps to reveal the Divinity in mathematics through right-triangles, which are composed of three sides measuring Three, Six and Nine (in ratio) respectively. But what is the mysterious enigma of Nine? Why does it continue to surface time and time again throughout the ages?

In the human experience, everything perceived is always in a constant state of motion and vibration. Even in solid matter, atoms are constantly moving; their building blocks constantly swirling around the other. The most solid matter consists of more space than it does fundamental building blocks, thus creating the illusion of solid matter. Everything from the smallest observed particle to the greatest structure in creation has a specific vibratory resonance that holds the atomic structure in place. This vibratory resonance creates the energy grid that is manifested from All That Is but is simultaneously the observable symptom of the energy grid in motion. The vibratory resonance reaches well below the audible spectrum and increases in equidistant proportion into the audible spectrum, above the audible spectrum and eventually into and out of the visual spectrum. The ever increasing rate of vibrations should be observed as a vibratory blanket through which methods of communication can occur within the senses of the human experience.

Part 3 | Song of the Spheres

The observed spectrums can be broken into octaves, Seven evenly spaced steps consisting of Twelve divisions – which should be observed as an equidistant bundle of earthly-defined frequencies that move in Divine Ratio & Proportion to each adjacent group of frequencies when observed linearly. But why Seven? And why Twelve Divisions? Oh, sweet Seed of Life, within You houses all of the answers to questions unanswered.

To fully understand the Pattern of Seven, it is important to explore how the Seed of Life is created. The Seed of Life is formed from Eight interlocked spheres which holds within it the Divine Seed. When the Seed of Life is observed from one side of the three-dimensional shape, only four spheres are directly observable. These four spheres should be numbered in the following order: the top-right sphere, the bottom-right sphere, the top-left sphere, and, finally, the bottom-left sphere. Now envision the other set of four interlocked spheres directly behind the observable four. Without adjusting perspective, observe these spheres as a second layer behind the first – whereby the first layer of four becomes completely transparent for this explanation. On this backside layer of spheres, the top-right sphere is the sixth, the bottom-right sphere is the seventh, the top-left sphere is the eighth, and the bottom-left sphere is the ninth. The fifth sphere is the Divine Seed located in the center.

When the cube of Eight spheres is rotated counterclockwise 45°, the first sphere located at the top of the shape of a diamond and the first, the left-most sphere is the third sphere, the right-most sphere is the second, and the bottom sphere is

Secrets

the fourth sphere. Now, when the first sphere is pulled down 45° over an imaginary three-dimensional Y-axis, the top-most sphere will be revealed as the sixth. The new sphere that appears in the top-left location (directly above the third sphere) is the eighth. The new sphere that appears in the top-right location (directly above the second sphere) is the seventh. As observed, the Fifth sphere is hidden within the center – the Divine Seed. The sphere located directly behind the Divine Seed is the Ninth Sphere and will henceforth be called the Octaval Sphere. To observe the manner in which each sphere is sequentially connected, envision a line that connects from one sphere's center point to the next in the order through which has been assigned to the spheres. One should observe that each observable sphere of the Seed of Life connects directly to another observable sphere in sequence except that the fourth sphere connects to the sixth, and the ninth sphere to the first. The pattern that emerges when traversing the observable spheres of the Seed of Life is as follows: from the first sphere to the second equals ONE. From the second sphere to the third equals ONE. From the third sphere to the fourth equals ONE. From the fourth sphere to the sixth (because the fifth sphere is hidden and the vector must traverse the fifth sphere to reach the sixth) equals TWO. From the sixth sphere to the seventh equals ONE. From the seventh sphere to the eighth sphere equals ONE. From the eighth sphere to the ninth equals TWO for a very special reason and shall henceforth be called the Octaval Sphere.. It is important to observe that the ninth sphere exists in three-dimensional space, but is not directly ob-

Part 3 | Song of the Spheres

servable from the centered viewpoint of the Seed of Life, thus the ninth sphere is tantamount to the first sphere. From the eighth sphere to the ninth sphere, the sequence is automatically closed because the beginning and end are tantamount to each other, both bound by the Divine Seed – thereby completing the Circle of Nine. It is important to observe that the vector from the eighth sphere traverses two directions simultaneously. It equals ONE when connecting the eighth sphere to the ninth and ALSO equals ONE when connecting the eight sphere to the first sphere (since this is the observable sphere). Thus ONE plus ONE equals TWO. The fully notated pattern is this: one, one, one, two, one, one, two. This pattern shall henceforth be called the Divine Pattern of Seven.

Because Nine spheres are observed as Seven, the Seventh bundle of Side Nine from the principles of Divine Ratios & Proportions should be used to understand the material world as observed through the human experience. The Seventh bundle of Side Nine consists of the numbers 174, 285, 396, 417, 528, 639, 741, 852, and 963. When these numbers are used to understand the ratios of all that is observable within the human experience, only Seven numbers will become manifest. These Seven numbers emerge from the Divine Pattern of Seven and are equivalent to the Seven steps within the octave. From the Seventh bundle of Side Nine, the observable number groups include the first, second, third, fourth, sixth, seventh, and eighth groups (the same as the observable spheres of the Seed of Life). The fifth group is unable to be directly observed within the human experience because it is tanta-

Secrets

mount to the Divine Seed (the center of the Divine Ratios to the center-most sphere). The Octaval Sphere is tantamount to the Ninth position, 963, and should be understood as the location of the pivot point that transcends bundles into the next sequential octave.

    Within the audible spectrum, the octave of a musical scale is traditionally notated through the first Seven letters of the alphabet – A through G. These letters also contain subdivisions that create equidistance in observable sound. These subdivisions are known as half steps, of which there are Twelve within the observable octave. The complete list of potential notes in an octave is: A, A#, B, C, C#, D, D#, E, F, F#, G, G#. Understand that for something to be observed as Equidistant through the human experience, the potential of Twelve notes must be reduced to Seven notes which observe the following pattern: whole step, whole step, half step, whole step, whole step, whole step. To move into the next octave, a half step is the equidistant space between the last note of the octave and the first note of the next sequential octave. So, if one is to start on the letter A, the Seven notes that will be played in Equidistance within an octave are: A, B (due to the whole step), C# (due to the whole step), D (due to the half step), E (due to the whole step), F# (due to the whole step), G# (due to the whole step). If one is to start on the note of C, the Seven notes that will be played in Equidistance within the octave are: C, D (due to the whole step), E (due to the whole step), F (due to the half step), G (due to the whole step), A (due to the whole step), B (due to the whole step). Thus, the Pattern

Part 3 | Song of the Spheres

of Seven has become manifest in observance as: whole step, whole step, half step, whole step, whole step, whole step, half step. This pattern shall henceforth be called the Observable Pattern of Seven.

Now that the Pattern of Seven has been observed in the human experience, it is important to understand why the Pattern of Seven must exist for Equidistance to be observed within the human experience. This understanding is revealed through the Seed of Life. The Twelve edges of a cube (tantamount to 12 potential notes in an octave) are formed from Nine spheres that manifest as the central Seven interlocking circles of the Seed of Life (as can be observed in a two-dimensional line drawing). The Divine Seed is the sphere located in the center of the Seed of Life whereas the center of the Nine number groups of Divine Ratios and Proportions is the fifth position. The ninth position of the number group is equivalent to the Octaval Sphere. The Divine Pattern of Seven follows the Observable Pattern of Seven through the same pattern of whole steps and half steps. However, before the patterns can be understood as one, it is important to observe that a half step of sound in the Observable Pattern of Seven appears equidistant to the human ear as a whole step because that particular note position has TWICE the amount of Ethereal Potential within HALF of the observed, mathematical space which has become manifest in the human experience (hence Nine spheres observed as Seven, with Two hidden within). Since a mathematical half step is tantamount in position to the position of TWO within the Divine Pattern of

Secrets

Seven, it means that it carries the same amount of observable potential in half of the observable space. Something that is observed as equal in spacing in the human experience is not always measured as equal through mathematics and physics.

Within Divine Ratios & Proportions, each number group is equidistant to the next within each bundle. So if each number is observed as representing a sphere of even proportion – the fifth number group represents the Divine Seed and the ninth number group represents the Octaval Sphere. So by skipping over the Fifth and Ninth spheres, the pattern that emerges from the Seven observable spheres is the following: whole step, whole step, whole step, whole step, two steps, whole step, whole step, whole step (with two steps ascending into the next fractal). The Pattern of Seven as observed through the Divine Ratios & Proportion of the Seventh bundle of Side Nine is constructed as follows: 174, 285, 396, 417, 639, 741, 852 which follows a pattern similar to the observable Pattern of Seven. In two separate instances, two spheres of Ethereal Potential are represented within Half the amount of space observable in the human experience. When the observable Pattern of Seven in the musical scale is aligned with the Pattern of Seven of Divine Ratio & Proportion, the pattern is as follows: 639, 741 (due to the whole step), 852 (due to the whole step), 174 (due to the half step), 285 (due to the whole step), 396 (due to the whole step), and 417 (due to the whole step). The next sequential step would be a half step into the next octave. The alignment of the Observable Pattern of Sev-

Part 3 | Song of the Spheres

en and the Divine Pattern of Seven shall henceforth be known as the Pattern of Seven.

Now that the Pattern of Seven has been aligned to the Seventh bundle of Side 9, an even more important pattern emerges. As previously discussed, the twisting motion of the Great Ethereal Machine affects each bundle at different locations along the number groups. From the Seventh bundle of Side Nine, the twist in Divine Ratio & Proportion occurs between the Third and Fourth number groups, 396 and 417. This should be observed as a pinch in the Equidistant Bouquet that creates a starting point for mathematics and physics in the human experience. Since everything observable is always relative to each other, there must be a starting point for everything to maintain harmony and balance in the human experience. To understand this concept, envision an orchestra where every instrument is perfectly tuned with itself, but each instrument is tuned to a different baseline. The same string played among twelve violin players could have twelve different pitches because they are not tuned with a standard baseline in mind. Within modern music, 440 hertz (cycles per second) is used to define how the note of "A" should sound (though 440 hertz was arbitrarily determined by popular consensus). When A is tuned to a universal frequency, every other note can be tuned in ratio and proportion to this baseline.

With the understanding that the number group of 417 can now be used as a starting point for all baselines to any measurable part of the vibratory spectrum, observe that the note of A in the musical scale should be tuned to 417 hertz. The reason

Secrets

that the number can transcend Divine Ratios & Proportions into mathematics within the human experience is because the definition of hertz yields to the same equidistant principles of measurement as those in Divine Ratios & Proportions. "Hertz" is measured as one full rotation around an axis over one unit of time. Therefore, measuring in hertz is an attempt to measure on the spherical principle of Divine Equidistance. So by starting with the note of "A" at 417 hertz and placing "A" at the first position of the Seventh bundle of Side Nine (174), it is possible to define the baseline key of the spectrums for the human experience.

If the note of "A" begins with the Pattern of Seven at the first position (174), the notes that would complete the octave are as follows: A, B (whole step), C# (whole step), D# (whole step), E (half step), F# (whole step), G# (whole step). This group of seven notes produces the Key of E as known within musical theory. It is no coincidence that "A" is the Fourth note in the Key of E, for the pinch in the Equidistant Bouquet indicates that the fourth position is the starting point for baselines. The baseline vibratory Key of Earth is observed as the Key of E where the baseline note of "A" must be tuned to 417 hertz. While the current example falls within the audible spectrum, the principles of octaves transcend into all other parts of the measurable spectrum – again manifesting for easy observance within the visual portion of the spectrum.

If one is to take the observable baseline of 417 hertz and add Twelve zeros to the end of the number, the number of 417×10^{12} is not, coincidentally, also the lowest observable fre-

Part 3 | Song of the Spheres

quency of color in the visible spectrum (which falls along the event-horizon of infra-red and red light). A prism splits white light into Seven observable colors: Red, Orange, Yellow, Green, Blue, Indigo, Violet. These colors follow the same Pattern of Seven, but because these are the only observable pure colors in a prism's spectrum, The Hidden can be found within the Divine Seed and the Octaval Sphere. This means that Red is tantamount to the note of "A" where "A" equals 417 hertz. Colors are not traditionally represented by hertz because of the complexity in notation (417×10^{12}). Instead, the preferred unit of measurement in modern times is nanometers. When hertz is converted into nanometers, the color Red receives a baseline wavelength of 718.93 nanometers. Nothing has changed through the equation except for the method of notation being the measurement of wavelength instead of the measurement of frequency. By understanding that the color Red must baseline at 718.93 nanometers and is tantamount to the note of "A" at 417 hertz in the Key of E, the remainder of the Seven colors can be specifically defined.

 Mathematically, an octave is measured to be the doubling or halving of a baseline frequency. So, the note of "A" has upper octaves of 834 hertz, 1668 hertz, 3336 hertz etc. These numbers mathematically will move upward throughout the audible part of the spectrum. But, to measure the frequencies of the relative Seven notes in the spectrum, an octave has to be divided by 12 to get the mathematical spacing of each half step, then applied to the Pattern of Seven to produce the note's frequencies. The notes in the example octave for the Key of E

Secrets

are as follows: E as 312.3970255 hertz, F# as 350.6538052 hertz, G# as 371.5047655 hertz, A as 417 hertz, B as 468.0666741 hertz, C# as 525.3870778 hertz, D# as 589.7270555 hertz, E (octave above) as 624.7940511 hertz. Therefore, by taking each number and adding Twelve zeros to the end and converting to nanometers, the corresponding colors of the spectrum become manifest. E as 312.3970255 hertz is in Divine Ratio to Blue at 479.83 nanometers; F# as 350.6538052 hertz is in Divine Ratio to Indigo at 427.48 nanometers; G# as 371.5047655 hertz is in Divine Ratio to Violet at 403.48 nanometers; A as 417 hertz is in Divine Ratio to Red at 718.93 nanometers; B as 468.0666741 hertz is in Divine Ratio to Orange at 640.49 nanometers; C# as 525.3870778 hertz is in Divine Ratio to Yellow at 570.61 nanometers; D# as 589.7270555 hertz is in Divine Ratio to Green at 508.36 nanometers; E (octave above) as 624.7940511 hertz is in Divine Ratio to Blue at 479.83 nanometers. So, this means that not only is the baseline Key of Earth the Key of E (assuming "A" tuned to 417 hertz), it is visually baselined to the color Blue – 479.83 nanometers to be exact.

All of the mathematical constructs of nanometers for the visible spectrum are direct translations from hertz to the twelfth power. The Pattern of Seven is not limited to just the visible and audible portions of the spectrum, but recurs throughout all Divinely-based measurements in the human experience. Now that the Pattern of Seven has been observed in both the audible and visual portions of the spectrum, it is important to observe that the baseline number group of Side

Part 3 | Song of the Spheres

Nine is also a product of 139 (a prime number) x 3. Earth is the Third planet from the Sun and observed through the construct of Three dimensions. The Divinity in the number Three will continue to resurface in All That Is, but it is important to take notice of how the numbers in Divine Ratios & Proportions occur through the manifestation of the human experience.

Though it took quite a bit of explanation to describe how Seven and Nine interrelate within the human experience through Divine Ratios & Proportion, it should now be much easier to understand the significance of the Two hidden spheres: the Divine Seed and the Octaval Sphere. These Two spheres shall henceforth be known as The Hidden due to the manner in which the twist in perspective of the Nine spheres hides the Two spheres from view in the Seed of Life. Everything observable will always manifest in Seven divisions but should always be understood to exist on the strength of all Nine spheres, for the sum of Seven is tantamount to the sum of Nine.

Within music, The Hidden occurs between the third and fourth notes and the seventh and eighth notes (the octave). The corresponding earthly interpretations of the frequencies and colors between the audible and visual portions of the spectrum for The Hidden are as follows: the Octaval Sphere as 410.34 hertz which is in Divine Ratio to Midnight-Red at 730.6 nanometers; the Divine Seed as 607.2605533 hertz which is in Divine Ratio to Azure at 493.68 nanometers. Because of the positional locations of The Hidden within the Key

Secrets

of E, the embodiment of the wavelengths of Azure shall henceforth be called the location of the Ninth Ray in the human experience even though it is the fifth position in the Seventh bundle of the Side of Nine. The Ninth Ray and all of its splendor is both accessible and inaccessible, based on perspective, to all who seek to understand the hidden message which is held within these words, through which will yield a ripple within the resonance of Divinity's Calling.

It is also important to observe how the locations of The Hidden within the musical scale occurs in very unique tonal positions, which transcend into manifestations and motions of vibratory states as witnessed within the human experience. When a group of Three notes is played together in the positions of the root note, the third note in sequence, and the fifth note in sequence, a chord is produced. However, there are variations of the Three notes that can make a chord sound "suspended." The "suspension" sounds to the observer as motion between two points. Without a resolution to the "suspended" chord, the observer is left feeling as if the sequence of notes is unfinished. The manner in which a chord manifests as "suspended" is to include the root note, the fourth note, and the fifth note. Regardless of the chord that is played, this combination of positions of notes will always create the "suspended" motion within the chord. It should be observed that the distance between the third and fourth notes in a chord traverse one of the locations of The Hidden. This location carries twice the amount of Ethereal Potential housed within The Hidden, so by traversing the location of The Octaval Sphere

Part 3 | Song of the Spheres

within The Hidden of the audible spectrum, the potential is manifest to the observer as unresolved motion. The other location of The Hidden is found between the seventh note and the octave. When a chord is played and includes the Seventh note, a chord called a Major Seventh is created. This chord has a Divine stillness manifest in sound. This chord sounds audibly more beautiful than if the Seventh note had not been added. When the seventh note is added, the chord consists of the last note of the chordal octave as well as the root (octave). This combination of notes traverses the Divine Seed that resides within The Hidden. Major Seventh chords are found most frequently in modern religious songs unbeknownst to the observer as to why the chord fits perfectly within the context of spiritual music. Henceforth it should be known that the Major 7th chord reveals the Divine Seed in The Hidden, and the suspended 4th chord reveals the Octaval Sphere.

One shall find that the locations of the Octaval Sphere and the Divine Seed of The Hidden do not hold within them magic as defined by the human experience, but instead should be understood as locations that hold the potential for an inner call to a Divine Gateway housed within each and every person – through which anything is possible. For nothing manifest in the human experience actually exists as understood in the human experience, but exists as potential from whence it was formed. The lens of the observer must bear humble witness as the lens of the observed to understand that the human experience is only finite through one direction of the lens. The Divine Gateway is accessible to all of those who strip them-

Secrets

selves of everything manifest in the human experience and humble themselves like unto a child in the eyes of God, the Almighty Creator. Only through His Grace and Wisdom shall ye be allowed access unto Thee.

Of Movement Through Equidistance

The shortest distance between two conceived points in the great expanse of All is the Fibonacci sequence – or better understood conceptually within the human experience as the three-dimensional representation of the Fibonacci sequence: a point spinning at a relative rate to the tangential arc created from an equidistant structure. All three Sides of the Great Ethereal Machine, when folded upon each other, represent the Divine Machine. The mechanism uses the motion of right-triangle vertices across the three planes that are folded onto each other through which each number group represents a tangential point in three-dimensional space used for a curve to travel. This can be visually manifested through understanding the principles of fluid dynamics. It can be seen in the cosmos in the spiraling of galaxies. It can be seen within nature – in the nautilus shell, the pinecone, the flowers, the trees, the human body, and through all that can be observed in the human experience.

It should be noted that movement through equidistance occurs in 45° increments to the observer. It is important to re-

Secrets

member that everything within the Equidistant Bouquet must be observed as the observer as well as the observed. The natural structure of equidistant spheres and the change of the observer's perspective causes great difficulty in transcending this form of motion into three-dimensional space, mathematics, or even into simple words. But, the most important takeaway is that everything travels in a corkscrew-like manner, represented by left-handed and right-handed polarization along a Fibonacci arc. Again, the best illustration of this in earthly manifestation is through the principles of vortex mathematics found within the study of fluid dynamics.

Of Ancient Mathematics

The fundamental truths held within ancient mathematics are often thought to be found within the expression of geometry. The term associated with this particular form of geometry is "sacred geometry" because it is based upon divine principles. However, even when the principles of this form of geometry are understood, mathematicians are often left with more questions than answers. Simply speaking, the questions beg for answers surrounding the irrationality of concepts like Phi, Pi, Avogadro's Number, etc. Questions resonate as to *why* the ancients used certain angles within their construction. The mathematics used to understand *how* these ancient civilizations arrived at the numbers has never been in question. The question as to *why* the ancients chose to use this form of mathematics has been a question left unanswered for ages.

The answer to this question is housed within the words of this book. The secrets to ancient mathematics are founded upon the principles of the Eight-Sphere Cube and the Song of the Spheres. Geometry is a two-dimensional expression of an incomprehensible Equidistant Bouquet. Lines and circles are the best representations to rationalizing the irrationality of the fundamental principle of Equidistance. Everything – without

Secrets

exception – is founded on the principle of spheres and the fabric created through the Equidistant Bouquet. To understand these principles, an educated person of rational mind must set aside all preconceived notions of how mechanics work in a binary way so that the grand beauty of the irrational can be revealed. Only upon understanding the principles discussed in the irrational, can a person begin to mathematically define rules and logic that coexist with irrational equidistance. This is truly the only means by which ancient mathematics can be understood.

While it would be laborious to examine all of the principles of irrational equidistance, the same fundamental principle from one example can be used in understanding all other irrational principles. The following example illustrates how a specific set of numbers and ratios used throughout ancient cultures reveals the earthly manifestation of rationality to an irrational concept. This type of earthly rationality can only be understood through visualizing the irrational mathematics of the Eight-Sphere Cube.

To begin, let's visualize the front face of four interlocking spheres that form the side of the Eight-Sphere Cube. Now, imagine pulling the top-right sphere horizontally 45° to the left so that the "edge" of the cube is now in the center of the observer's field of view, revealing both sides of the cube. Next, the same sphere used to pivot the cube should be pulled downward 45° to reveal the top of the Eight-Sphere Cube. The illusion created in a two-dimensional model is the innermost portion to the diagram of the Flower of Life.

Part 3 | Song of the Spheres

The next part is the most important part to understand. For, just as the cube has been pulled 45° in equidistance, the angles created (when measured from the diameters of the spheres) are different than the angles of the motion of the spheres used to create the shape. To visualize how lines and spheres in equidistance differ in measurement, it is important to assign units of measurement to the spheres in order to understand ancient mathematics.

If one is to visualize each sphere as having a diameter of five units each, the overall size of the cube created by the diameters of the spheres would be 5x5x5. However, the simple rotation of the spheres that allows the observer to view the cube along the edge creates a shape that is not mathematically possible. From the viewpoint of the edge, the visible portion of the top-most, central-axis sphere would measure 2.5 units (half of the diameter). This means that the dimensions to an imagined triangle created by the top slope of the cube would measure five units from the front layer of spheres to the second layer of spheres (when measured from the lines created by the diameters). The height of the top part of the triangle would be 2.5 units because only half of the diameter of the sphere is visible. The final portion of the triangle (the hypotenuse) would also measure five units because the spheres must maintain equidistance. Mathematically, this is an impossible shape. It cannot be created in two-dimensional or three-dimensional space. So the greater question is how do these angles translate into quantifiable mathematics?

Secrets

Due to the impossible nature of creating tangible reproductions from an impossible shape, the reproduction must be created using earthly mathematics. If the top visible portion of the cube measures 2.5 units, and the distance from the front layer of spheres to the second layer of spheres measures five units, and the angle created by those two joining measurements is 90°, the Pythagorean Theorem states that the hypotenuse could be determined by using the following formula: $2.5^2 + 5^2 = x^2$. Overall, this means the hypotenuse would measure 5.5901 units. Already, this is an impossible principle in equidistance, but possible to manifest in the earthly experience. So if mankind were to attempt to recreate just this top portion of the Eight-Sphere Cube on Earth, these are the numbers that must be used.

If it is understood that a cube has four sides, then it stands to reason that the illusion of the Eight-Sphere Cube (when viewed from each side) would manifest in earthly form as a pyramid when each viewpoint is superimposed upon each other. At the most basic level, a pyramid is just the smallest recreatable portion of the Equidistant Bouquet. To determine the angles, it is important to use the measurements we calculated from before. If the hypotenuse is 5.5901 units and the opposite side is 2.5 units, we can apply the formula:

$$\sin^{-1}(2.5/5.5901) \text{ equals } 26.565°.$$

The angle of 26.565° is based on the concept of a triangle having 180°. And while this is true in earthly mathematics, a

Part 3 | Song of the Spheres

sphere is comprised of 360°, so the number must be doubled to represent the angle perceived in the human experience. Therefore, 26.565° x 2 = 53.13°. This is the precise angle used in both the Khafre pyramid in Egypt and the Chichén Itza pyramid found on the Yucatan Peninsula. Additionally, this particular number recurs throughout Pythagorean mathematics in the concept of the 3-4-5 right triangle. With further exploration of the mathematics of equidistant spheres, the knowledge used by the ancients can be unveiled.

As it has just been demonstrated, the truths hidden within the principles of ancient mathematics are based on the irrationality of the illusion of shapes formed within the Equidistant Bouquet. These principles transcend irrationality into rational concepts, but most importantly answer *why* ancient mathematics was used in the creation of ancient megalithic architecture and carries such a divine connotation in use and practicality. The concept of equidistance and the angle of the observer versus the angle of the observed create a pulse – a breath within the motion. The understanding of breath, life, and many more answers can also be found within the information contained in this specific chapter – and, most importantly, within the entirety of this book – but the purpose of these words is to serve as a guidepost for those seeking answers and reason. Further answers can be brought to light upon deeper exploration of the concepts discussed within this book and the application of the principles of equidistance in earthly mathematics and creation.

Of The Eight-Sphere Cube

As defined in the chapter entitled "Of The Equidistant Bouquet," the Flower of Life is a 2-dimensional drawing of a 3-dimensional concept that cannot be drawn in the human experience. Furthermore, in the chapter entitled "Of Seven & The Hidden Within The Nine," the application of the Flower of Life's Divine Ratios and Proportions are demonstrated in the manifestation of light and sound in the human experience. So with those two principles defined, it is now important to understand the additional divinity of the Eight-Sphere Cube.

To begin, let's visualize the front face of 4 interlocking spheres that form the side of the Eight-Sphere Cube. Now let's number the spheres. The number for the top-right sphere is "one," the bottom-right sphere is "two," the top-left sphere is "three," and the bottom-left sphere is "four." Now visualize the second set of four interlocking spheres immediately behind the front face of the Eight-Sphere Cube. Without changing the viewpoint or observer's perspective, the number of the top-back-right sphere is "six," the bottom-back-right sphere is "seven," the top-back-left sphere is "eight," and the bottom-back-left sphere is "nine." Finally, envision a central sphere that is housed within the eight spheres. This sphere is called the Divine Seed and should be numbered "five." This is the same diagram used to illustrate the hidden spheres in "Of Seven & The Hidden Within The Nine."

Now that the Eight-Sphere Cube has been numbered, it is important to point out that by tracing the numerical pattern of the spheres sequentially, a sine wave is created. It should be observed that the tracing of the pattern of the spheres should occur along the arcs and tangents of the spheres, creating a further twisting in the motion. This is the principal of the motion inside of the Seed of Life. This is also the foundational principal used in the origins of written language. This foundational principle is demonstrated in how Hebrew is read right to left. Additionally, to understand the vowels and pronunciations of words, markings are made above and below the letters to illustrate how the letters are joined and pronounced. So Hebrew is really read in a sine wave pattern, from right to left, beginning at the top of the first letter, proceeding through the letter itself, reaching the bottom of the letter where any marking would be, proceeding to the top of the second letter in search of any markings, through the second letter and to the bottom of the letter where further markings may reside, et cetera. This pattern continues through the entire written language. These same principals are not limited to Hebrew and span the globe in the origins of most ancient languages.

Now that this sine wave pattern has been understood, let's view the cube along the edge. Applying the principles defined

Part 3 | Song of the Spheres

in the chapter entitled "Of Ancient Mathematics," the top-right sphere (number one), should be pulled horizontally 45° to the left so that the "edge" of the cube is not in the center of the observer, revealing both sides. Now, the same sphere used to pivot the cube (the number one sphere) should now be pulled down 45° to reveal the top of the Eight-Sphere Cube. While, this is the visualization to get us to this point, it is important to reveal that the illusion created by transparent spheres means that the "cube" that is visualized exists in multiple states at once. This is the optical illusion created by the lines of each sphere's radius. But for now, we are just going to observe the pattern.

The spheres should now appear as follows: the center sphere is ONE; the sphere located North of the central sphere is sphere EIGHT; the sphere located Northeast from the central sphere is sphere SIX; the sphere located Southeast of the central sphere is sphere SEVEN; the sphere located South of the central sphere is sphere TWO; the sphere located Southwest of the central sphere is sphere FOUR; finally, the Northwest sphere is sphere THREE. With this pattern it is important now to see that if a vector is drawn through each of the alignments of three spheres, all vectors will total the same number. The North-to-South vector totals ELEVEN (EIGHT + ONE + TWO). The Northwest-to-Southeast vector totals ELEVEN (THREE + ONE + SEVEN). The Northeast-to-Southwest vector totals ELEVEN (SIX + ONE + FOUR).

Now, it is important to understand that if the Eight-Sphere Cube were rotated to bring the right side of the Eight-

Secrets

Sphere Cube into the central view of the observer (without moving the alignment of the Eight-Sphere Cube in any way), the same pattern of the spheres still exists, but the numbering of the spheres has changed. This is extremely important to understand. So even though it may be laborious to read, it is important to write out how the divine properties of the Eight-Sphere Cube become manifest when properly understood by the observer.

From the *right side*, the observable spheres would be as follows: Center: SIX, North: THREE, Northeast: EIGHT, Southeast: NINE, South: SEVEN, Southwest: TWO, Northwest: ONE. The North-to-South vector totals SIXTEEN (THREE + SIX + SEVEN). The Northwest-to-Southeast vector totals SIXTEEN (ONE + SIX + NINE). The Northeast-to-Southwest vector totals SIXTEEN (EIGHT + SIX + TWO).

From the *left side*, the observable spheres would be as follows: Center: THREE, North: SIX, Northeast: ONE, Southeast: TWO, South: FOUR, Southwest: NINE, Northwest: EIGHT. The North-to-South vector totals THIRTEEN (SIX + THREE + FOUR). The Northwest-to-Southeast vector totals THIRTEEN (EIGHT + THREE + TWO). The Northeast-to-Southwest vector totals THIRTEEN (ONE + THREE + NINE).

From the *top side*, the observable spheres would be as follows: Center: EIGHT, North: NINE, Northeast: SEVEN, Southeast: SIX, South: ONE, Southwest: THREE, Northwest: FOUR. The North-to-South vector totals EIGHTEEN (NINE

Part 3 | Song of the Spheres

+ EIGHT + ONE). The Northwest-to-Southeast vector totals EIGHTEEN (FOUR + EIGHT + SIX). The Northeast-to-Southwest vector totals EIGHTEEN (SEVEN + EIGHT + THREE).

From the *bottom side*, the observable spheres would be as follows: Center: TWO, North: ONE, Northeast: SIX, Southeast: SEVEN, South: NINE, Southwest: FOUR, Northwest: THREE. The North-to-South vector totals TWELVE (ONE + TWO + NINE). The Northwest-to-Southeast vector totals TWELVE (THREE + TWO + SEVEN). The Northeast-to-Southwest vector totals TWELVE (SIX + TWO + FOUR).

From the *back side*, the observable spheres would be as follows: Center: NINE, North: EIGHT, Northeast: THREE, Southeast: FOUR, South: TWO, Southwest: SEVEN, Northwest: SIX. The North-to-South vector totals NINETEEN (EIGHT + NINE + TWO). The Northwest-to-Southeast vector totals NINETEEN (SIX + NINE + FOUR). The Northeast-to-Southwest vector totals NINETEEN (THREE + NINE + SEVEN).

It can now be seen that the sums of each of the sides of the Eight-Sphere Cube creates sums of ELEVEN, TWELVE, THIRTEEN, SIXTEEN, EIGHTEEN, and NINETEEN. Now let's draw a vector through the X, Y, and Z axes of the 3-dimensional space the illusion of the cube creates. How would the sums work? To answer this question, remember that the Divine Seed is hidden within the center of the Eight-Sphere Cube. This is the sphere numbered FIVE. In all cases, from every viewpoint, the X-axis will always add to FIFTEEN, the

Secrets

Y-axis will always add to FIFTEEN, and the Z-axis will always add to FIFTEEN. The vector of the observer's line-of-sight through the middle of the cube will, also, always total FIFTEEN.

Now let's take the faces of each side of the Eight-Sphere Cube and add the vectors on the faces. In this case, the first face we observe illustrates the Northeast sphere as ONE, the Southeast sphere as TWO, the Northwest sphere as THREE, and the Southwest sphere as FOUR. Remember that the Divine Seed is now observable in the middle (though hidden from view), so it will always be the center sphere on each face of the Eight-Sphere Cube. This means that the vectors only consist of Northwest-to-Southeast and Northeast-to-Southwest. In both cases, the vectors total TEN for the *front side*.

For the *right side*, the spheres are as follows: Center: FIVE, Northeast: SIX, Southeast: SEVEN, Northwest: ONE, Southwest: TWO. In both cases, the vectors add to THIRTEEN.

For the *left side*, the spheres are as follows: Center: FIVE, Northeast: THREE, Southeast: FOUR, Northwest: EIGHT, Southwest: NINE. In both cases, the vectors total SEVENTEEN.

For the *top side*, the spheres are as follows: Center: FIVE, Northeast: SIX, Southeast: ONE, Northwest: EIGHT, Southwest: THREE. In both cases, the vectors add to FOURTEEN.

Part 3 | Song of the Spheres

For the *bottom side*, the spheres are as follows: Center: FIVE, Northeast: TWO, Southeast: SEVEN, Northwest: FOUR, Southwest: NINE. In both cases, the vectors total SIXTEEN.

For the *back side*, the spheres are as follows: Center: FIVE, Northeast: EIGHT, Southeast: NINE, Northwest: SIX, Southwest: SEVEN. In both cases, the vectors add to TWENTY.

So, through the understanding of the summing of the vectors, it is sequentially possible to demonstrate the numbers ONE through NINE (in the numbering of the original spheres), TEN, ELEVEN, TWELVE, THIRTEEN, FOURTEEN, FIFTEEN, SIXTEEN, SEVENTEEN, EIGHTEEN, NINETEEN, and TWENTY. At this point, it is important to observe that the number of vertices in a dodecahedron is TWENTY. And just like the number of edges in the illusion of the cube created by the Eight-Sphere Cube is TWELVE, the number of faces of a dodecahedron is TWELVE. And just as FIVE is the numbering notation of the Divine Seed, the dodecahedron is created by the rotation of a cube FIVE times on a central axis. This is why the outermost understanding of the energy grid is a dodecahedron – for within the dodecahedron, is the motion of the Eight-Sphere Cube. TWENTY numeric sequences are the equivalent of three base-nine sequences of SEVEN. In the concepts of the TWENTY-TWO archetypes, the twenty-second archetype represents choice of direction, acceptance, and above all – Love.

Secrets

These are the secrets of the Eight-Sphere Cube. The motion of the observer with respect to the spheres should be seen as a corkscrew-like motion – a polarized motion within a tube encompassing the Eight-Sphere Cube. The motion of the spheres themselves can be derived from the mathematics formed from the geometry of the sums of the spheres. It is through this understanding that the mysteries of every manifestation in the human experience can be understood.

Of Gravity

Gravity should be observed as "the triangular coupling of a toroidal simplex." This is the word-for-word answer to the question the angels delivered to me. If the smallest concept of Anything That Can Be is an infinitely small sphere, the vector of motion should also be observed as circular/spherical. In the creation of the Divine Seed, the Seed of Life and the Flower of Life, three spheres must exist for anything to first manifest in the human experience. For if there is one, one must be two, and two must be three in order for the divine structure of equidistance to be understood. It is tantamount to the human experience being founded upon the mind, the body, and the spirit. So, in the understanding of three, gravity can be understood as the aetheric calling to the polarization created through the perfectly circular architecture of the Song of the Spheres. It is Unity. It is Love.

Requisition

The words encased in this book reveal the divine secrets of All That Is, All That Was, and All That Will Be. The Equidistant Bouquet is the most divine principle of His creation. It is the fundamental fabric of existence. Through the exploration of these concepts, the knowledge herein will give rise to understanding the world as seen through the eyes of man.

At first, it may seem as if the concepts in this book are esoteric or even some form of philosophical art. But, in truth, the concepts are fundamentally required to understand the starting point of this portion of existence. Understanding that the existence of a line is an idea and that a line is only the expression of the radius of a sphere will yield an endless fountain of knowledge for mankind's growth.

The bundle of spheres that form the Eight-Sphere Cube holds the key to the divine blueprint of mankind's three-dimensional illusion of existence. It is real. It is tangible. But, the reality is only manifest from perspective. For in equidistance, spheres are held together in perfect balance, ratio, and proportion. The explosion of perfection into the space that mankind understands through its senses, is bound specifically by the viewer's lens of perspective.

Secrets

To those who practice cryptography, numbers are found on each of the nine spheres, where the path of the viewer through the spheres can reveal the rationality to irrational numbers: the key to technology's best approach in attempting to create an unbreakable seal. Anything that is created can be unraveled more efficiently than the act of the creation itself, unless the creation was in thought.

To the scientists and chemists – the elements that comprise the periodic table are formed representations of divine thought. The elements can all be aligned to the Pillars of the Mind, Body, and Soul. Sequentially, they represent the letters of the alphabet at an atomic level. Hydrogen is the lightest element, but is unstable in the atmosphere. This is because Helium holds it in place. Think of this as Aleph and Beyt and how those two archetypes represent "strength" and "house." Together they form the word "father" which is the linguistic representation how a tent-pole holds up a body of cloth, and the body of cloth holds the tent-pole in place.

The element that has the most fundamental potential for energy is Lithium (hence Lithium's use in batteries). The third archetype of the Mind is Gimel, which represents overflowing abundance/wealth. This pattern can continue on through the periodic table. Once the first 22 elements have been covered, the concept of fractals (similar to octaves in music) is used.

Just by taking the time to understand the Pillars and the Spheres, it becomes very easy to see why the elements used in atomic weapons were chosen. This knowledge also helps to unravel answers to other such questions: Why is silicon the

Requisition

best element for electronics? Why do phosphorus and sulfur hold darker, demonic origin stories? Why is Carbon one of the primary elements of life? And why would Gold ever have been chosen as the most valued element, when other elements may be more rare?

    The Pillars hold the answers to these questions and answers to even more foundational scientific principles, such as the explanation of why the six fundamental elements of life must exist for life (as mankind understands it) to be. The number of the body is six. The number of divinity is seven.

    Scientists may continue to justify chemical reactions though the methods of their individual understanding. But scientific understanding could even be used as a tool to help society understand how words were formed from the original archetypes, and why words and names carry the meanings that they do. Everything is connected. And, it is all just a different representation of thought. The bindings of the elements are held together through the concepts of Earth, Wind, Fire, and Water, which is the framework to the Aether – or more appropriately understood as a representation of the Spirit within.

    To the musicians, music is a dance upon the spheres – a variation of the language to the divine. Melodies, harmonies, and counterpoints, are all expressions of a progression through the archetypes – an aural replication of the words to feelings within. Expressed vertically, horizontally, and diagonally in the motion of the song, words are formed from the spheres, thoughts held together through the notes of the song. The dynamics in speed, is a regulation to the expression of outward passion or inward desire and need.

To the artists – colors and pigments are just the same. They fall upon the boundaries of the spheres as they appear upon this plane. The wash of colors upon a canvas of white holds unfathomable reflections of the emotions being expressed through the hand. If music is a complex story told simultaneously in three directions and in dynamics, then art should be seen as an endless story, shortened only in plotline by the edges of the canvas. From right-to-left, left-to-right, top-to-bottom, bottom-to-top, and every diagonal in between – the flow of colors, lines, and arcs are the words to an epic journey of the spheres.

To the dancers, martial artists, and those who practice motion within the world – the movements all form a divine conversation in thought. The motion is an articulate path through the spheres. Where song and pigment express words, dance and motion express the roller-coaster ride through the words that are formed. It is the perspective of the arc, a journey through the above and through the below. And in the end, it will always return to the start.

These are the seeds to the garden of knowledge. These are not stones that build a path to the Glorious Divine. Seeds left untended will never wither away, for life will always be found within. But to view these words as stones is to believe that man can build and create a Glorious Divine. Truth is found within the soul. It is not something that can be created nor something that can be reproduced. It is only through humility as a slave

Requisition

to a master, that water is provided to help the seed grow in His Garden.

The Tower of Babel was once destroyed. The story was great enough to transcend from generations lost to generations found. It is important to understand that those who choose to use these seeds as stones will not prevail. Stones will crumble. Towers will fall. Without submission to the spirit, a person is only building a sandcastle in a giant sandbox so they may one day learn this mighty lesson. The sun will render the castle dry. The wind will wither it away. The tide will wash its support from its foundation below. And, inevitably, a storm will come and destroy that which was made. Only the sand remains. Only the sand sustains.

...

This is His beginning and His end, All That Was and All That Will Be. This is the Divine Architecture of His Glory. Praises unto Him, forever unto Eternity.

...

www.ingramcontent.com/pod-product-compliance
Lightning Source LLC
Chambersburg PA
CBHW021151080526
44588CB00008B/295